BUDDHIST BELIEFS AND ISSUES

Michael Keene

Badger

CONTENTS

You will find out

- About the birth of the Buddha.
- About the wife and son of the Buddha.
- The four sights that changed the Buddha's life.

In the glossary

Benares

Buddha

Siddhartha Gautama

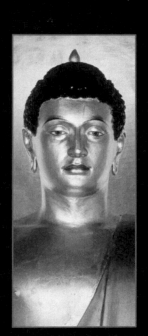

Siddhartha Gautama, who later came to be called the **Buddha**, was the founder of Buddhism. The son of a rajah [king], he was born about 560 BCE and died at the age of eighty. He was born in north-eastern India, at a time when that part of the world was a great centre of Hindu learning and culture.

THE BIRTH OF SIDDHARTHA GAUTAMA

As happens with the founders of many religions, all kinds of legends have sprung up around the birth of Gautama. One legend describes how his mother [Maya] dreamed that a white elephant entered her womb and, ten months later, she gave birth to a baby on the day of the full moon in May.

The earth trembled and supernatural beings were also present at Gautama's birth. His mother died seven days after – because, as legend says, a woman who has given birth to the Buddha cannot serve any other useful purpose.

The child was given two names:

- Siddhartha – meaning 'he who has reached his goal'.
- Gautama, after a famous teacher from whom he was descended.

The young prince was brought up by his aunt, in the greatest possible luxury. His father made sure of this because, when he was named, a wise man had told him that his son would either become a ruler or a wandering holy man. To make sure that he became a ruler, his father tried to remove from him any outside influence or temptation.

This is how Siddhartha Gautama described his early life:

A *"I was spoiled, very spoiled. I anointed myself with only Benares sandalwood and dressed only in Benares cloth. Day and night a white sunshade was held over me. I had a palace for the winter, one for the summer and one for the rainy season. In the four months of the rainy season I did not leave the palace at all and I was surrounded by female musicians."*

The Buddha

TAKE TIME TO THINK

a) Why do you think that the birth of great religious founders is usually surrounded by miraculous happenings?

b) What do such legends tell you about the importance of the person?

c) Can you think of one legend that is attached to the birth of a religious founder other than the Buddha?

The early life of the Buddha was one of great luxury until four sights changed the course of his life.

THE FOUR EXPERIENCES [SIGHTS]

The young prince married a girl called Gopa [or Yashodara] who was, according to legend, outstanding for her beauty, modesty and breeding. When Gautama had a son, however, he called him Rahula [chains]. This was because, in the midst of all his luxury, he felt that he was in chains. He decided to leave everything and become homeless.

Before leaving home, however, Siddhartha had four experiences that changed his life:

- He saw a frail old man – which showed him how old age destroys memory, beauty and strength.
- He saw an invalid racked with pain – he was shocked to see pain and suffering and "trembled like the reflection of the moon in rippling water".
- He saw weeping mourners following a funeral procession – this was the first time he had encountered death.
- He met a wandering Hindu holy man, contented and joyful, travelling around with an alms bowl. He suddenly saw that all of life's pleasures and treasures were worthless.

What Siddhartha Gautama now longed for was true knowledge. He left his palace and family in the middle of the night and stole away to search for that sense of inner peace.

OVER TO **YOU** ▶▶▶

1 What did Siddhartha Gautama call his son and why?
2 a) What four experiences did Siddhatha Gautama have that totally changed his life?
   b) Why did each one of them have such a strong impact on him?
3 Have you had any experience that has had a very great impact on you? Describe it if you can.

UNIT 2
THE BUDDHA – THE ENLIGHTENED ONE

You will find out

- The ways of finding the truth that Siddhartha Gautama rejected.

- The steps by which Siddhartha Gautama reached enlightenment.

- What happened to the Buddha after he was enlightened.

In the glossary

Benares

Bodhissatva

Brahman

Buddha

Enlightenment

Four Noble Truths

Mara

Nibbana

Reincarnation

Siddhartha Gautama

Yoga

When the Buddha was enlightened, he could have entered paradise immediately.

After Siddhartha Gautama left home, he began searching for knowledge, as many Indian holy men also did at the time. He tried constant **yoga** exercises but they did not give him the knowledge he was looking for. For six years, he lived in extreme poverty and self-denial with five companions, but he was still dissatisfied. Finally, in desperation, he left his friends and sat beneath a bodhi tree to meditate.

SIDDHARTHA GAUTAMA IS ENLIGHTENED

Siddhartha Gautama sat beneath the tree, going into deeper and deeper meditation. During the next three nights, he went through three stages of **enlightenment** and resisted the temptations of **Mara** [the Evil One], who tried to persuade Gautama to enter **nibbana** [paradise] at once. By the end of the third night, he saw the whole truth of existence:

- On the first night of meditation, his previous lives all passed before him. You will discover more about the Buddhist belief in **reincarnation** in Unit 25.

- On the second night, he saw the cycle of birth, death and rebirth and recognised the law that governs it. This is how a later follower described this experience:

A "*During the second watch he saw that the death and rebirth of all living things depended on whether they had thought and done good or bad things during their lifetimes. He saw that the threat of death is always present and that creatures could never find a resting-place.*"

- On the third night, he came to understand the **Four Noble Truths** – the knowledge of suffering, the source of suffering, the removal of suffering and the way to remove suffering. These formed the basis of his teaching. You will find out more about the Four Noble Truths in Unit 7.

AFTER THE ENLIGHTENMENT

After Gautama's enlightenment, he became the Buddha – the Enlightened One – and he was asked by the high God, **Brahman**, three times to help others to enlightenment by teaching them. Someone who does this is called a **bodhissatva**. This is what the Buddha did.

He preached his first sermon at **Benares** and his five former companions became his first five disciples. Soon this number grew. People were convinced by the serene calm of the preacher.

Buddha sent them out to preach the good news. The Buddha travelled around India for 44 years, living as a beggar-monk. At the age of 80, however, he was taken ill during a meal and died in the town of **Kushinagara**. There are many legends surrounding his death. They describe his joyful entry into nibbana and the terrible earthquake that shook the earth during his cremation.

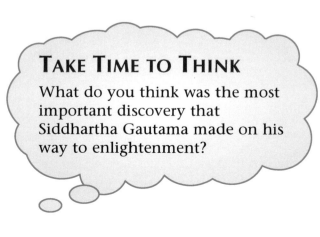

TAKE TIME TO THINK

What do you think was the most important discovery that Siddhartha Gautama made on his way to enlightenment?

OVER TO **YOU** ▶▶▶

1 Which ways of reaching the truth did the Buddha reject?
2 How did Siddhartha Gautama reach the truth?
3 A Buddhist said that: "The enlightenment of the Buddha was the most important event in history." Why do you think he said this?

BUDDHISM WORLDWIDE

You will find out

- The early spread of Buddhism.
- About Buddhism reaching the West.
- About the pillars of Emperor Ashoka.

In the glossary

Buddha

Dharma

Mahayana Buddhism

Pilgrimage

Theravada Buddhism

Buddhism began in northern India but soon spread further afield. Even during the lifetime of the Buddha, the new faith, under the drive of its founder, became very popular. Many were attracted to its message of finding a release from life's ills – especially from groups like the lower castes in Hindu society, who were despised by everyone else.

THE SPREAD OF BUDDHISM

From India, Buddhism soon spread to other countries. This particularly happened during the reign of Emperor Ashoka, who ruled over India between 268/9 BCE and 232 BCE. His own son and daughter became a Buddhist monk and nun. They took Buddhism to Sri Lanka. By the 9th century, it had become well established in China as well, before spreading to neighbouring countries.

CHECK IT OUT

Korea [4th century]

Burma [5th century]

Japan [6th century]

The spread of Buddhism

Thailand [5th century]

Laos [5th century]

Malaysia [5th century]

Cambodia [5th century]

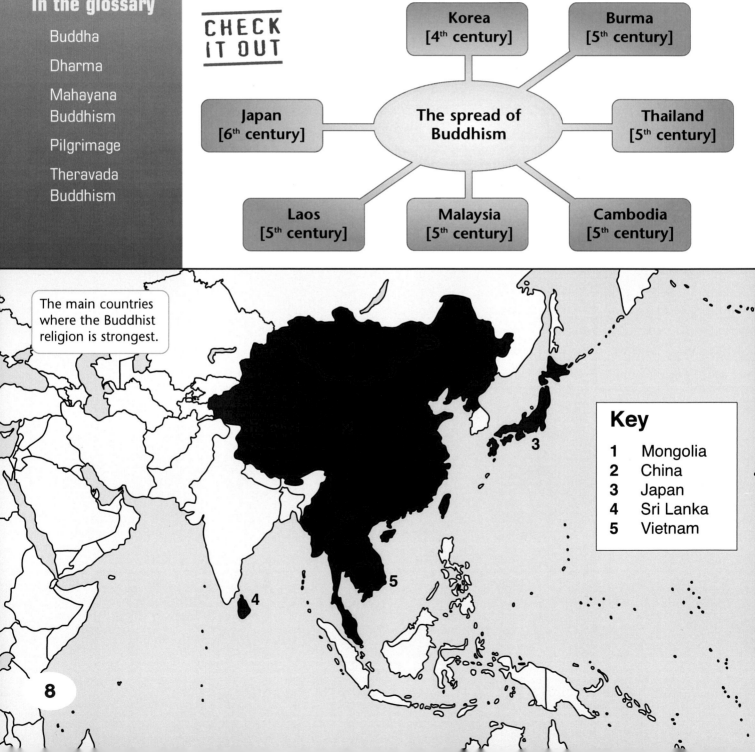

The main countries where the Buddhist religion is strongest.

Key

1 Mongolia
2 China
3 Japan
4 Sri Lanka
5 Vietnam

Buddhism did not reach the countries of the West, however, for centuries. It was not until the 19th century that it travelled from Japan to America. The first Buddhist missionary to arrive in Great Britain landed in 1893. Today, however, there are Buddhists in almost every country in the world.

EMPEROR ASHOKA'S PILLARS

Emperor Ashoka commanded that pillars should be erected in places where important events in the life of the Buddha took place – with writing on them to explain what those events were. He suggested to people that they should make **pilgrimages** to these places.

The emperor also ordered that many of the policies of his government should be displayed in this way – and many of these still remain. They show that Emperor Ashoka was a very enlightened ruler who tried to put the teachings of the Buddha into practice. One of these pillars reads:

A *"Beloved of the Gods [i.e. Ashoka] speaks thus: Father and Mother should be respected and so should elders. Kindness to living beings should be made strong and the truth should be spoken. In these ways the Dharma [Buddha's teachings] should be promoted. Likewise a teacher should be honoured by his pupils and proper manners should be shown to relations. This is the ancient rule that is conducive to long life. This one should act."*

Written by the scribe, Capala

BUDDHIST GROUPS

From a very early time, there were two separate Buddhist groups – the **Mahayana** and the **Theravada** Buddhists. You will find out more about these two groups and their different beliefs in Unit 4.

Later, there were smaller Buddhist groups as well. Two of these groups were the Tibetan and the Zen Buddhists. These groups still have their followers in many countries today. Buddhist customs, and particularly festivals, are celebrated in different ways in different countries.

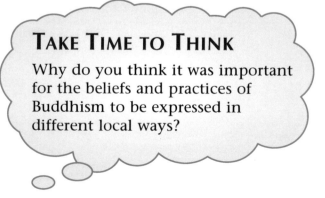

TAKE TIME TO THINK

Why do you think it was important for the beliefs and practices of Buddhism to be expressed in different local ways?

OVER TO **YOU** ▶▶▶

1 Put the words of Emperor Ashoka on the pillar into your own words.
2 How were the people encouraged to put the teachings of the Buddha into practice?

THE TWO MAIN SCHOOLS OF BUDDHISM

You will find out

- About Mahayana Buddhism.
- About Theravada Buddhism.
- About bodhissatvas.

In the glossary

Bodhissatva

Buddha

Enlightenment

Koan

Mahayana Buddhism

Mantra

Nibbana

Pali Canon

Sangha

Theravada Buddhism

The community of monks, the sangha, has played a very important part in the growth of Buddhism.

There are millions of Buddhists throughout the world. Although they all follow the teachings of the Buddha, they do not necessarily agree on the meaning of the different teachings. There are two different 'Schools' of Buddhism:

THERAVADA BUDDHISM

The word 'Theravada' means 'the teachings of the elders'. An elder is a teacher who is greatly respected. Theravada Buddhism is the form of Buddhism mainly found in Sri Lanka, Burma, Thailand and other parts of south-east Asia. Its teachings are based on scriptures called the **Pali Canon**, which Theravada Buddhists believe to be the most accurate record of what the Buddha said and did.

Theravada Buddhists believe that:

- The Buddha was only a man – one in a long succession of buddhas.
- Personal enlightenment can be reached only through following his example and teachings.
- Monks and nuns are freed from their domestic responsibilities. This means that they have the best chance of reaching nibbana.
- Householders achieve merit for a better future life by making offerings of food, clothes and money to the monks, but they stand little chance of reaching nibbana at the end of this life.

Theravada Buddhists do not pray to the Buddha.

TAKE TIME TO THINK

Why do you think that the sangha is so important to Buddhists?

Like this bodhissatva, the Buddha chose to remain on Earth after his enlightenment to help others to find the way.

BODHISSATVAS

Bodhissatvas are men and women who have reached enlightenment, so they could have entered nibbana. Instead, they chose to be reborn so that they could guide others to nibbana.

Bodhissatvas are filled with peace and joy because of the way they have trained their minds. There are a large number of them. Mahayana Buddhists pray to them for help in reaching enlightenment as well as help in their daily lives. They believe that any good Buddhist could become a bodhissatva in the future.

MAHAYANA BUDDHISM

The word 'Mahayana' means 'Great Vehicle'. This is a way of saying that there are many different ways of reaching nibbana. Mahayana Buddhists believe that there have been, and are, many buddhas.

Mahayana Buddhists believe that:

- People do not have to rely on their own efforts, or become a monk/nun, to reach nibbana. Instead, they are helped towards nibbana by many bodhissatvas and teachers [see below].
- The bodhissatvas and teachers help people reach nibbana by:

CHECK
IT OUT

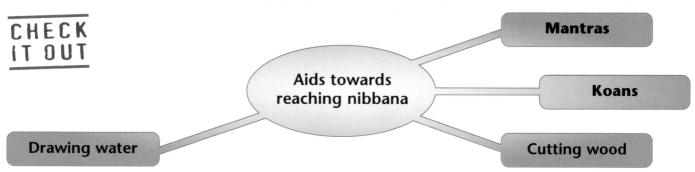

Aids towards reaching nibbana

Mantras

Koans

Cutting wood

Drawing water

- The **sangha**, the community of monks, are those who practise the teachings of the Buddha. The sangha has been responsible for keeping those teachings alive since the death of the Buddha.

Mahayana Buddhists believe that they can pray to the many buddhas and the bodhissatvas for help.

OVER TO YOU ▶▶▶

1 Here are some terms that are used in this section. Using the information that you have been given, and by carrying out some research of your own, write a paragraph to explain the meaning of:

a) Theravada Buddhism   b) Mahayana Buddhism   c) Bodhissatvas

2 Describe two ways in which the followers of Mahayana and Theravada Buddhism are different from each other.

BEING A BUDDHIST

AS INDIVIDUALS

In their daily lives, Buddhists try to follow the example and the teachings of the Buddha. They do this by accepting the Four Noble Truths [Unit 7] and following the **Eight-Fold Path** or the **Middle Way** [Unit 8]. This is a way of living between the two extremes of luxury and poverty. All Buddhists follow the **Five Precepts**, which means that they live without harming any living creature:

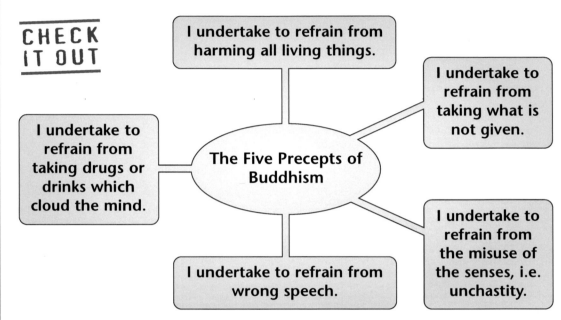

CHECK IT OUT

I undertake to refrain from harming all living things.

I undertake to refrain from taking what is not given.

I undertake to refrain from taking drugs or drinks which cloud the mind.

The Five Precepts of Buddhism

I undertake to refrain from the misuse of the senses, i.e. unchastity.

I undertake to refrain from wrong speech.

Buddhism teaches a very high standard of personal behaviour and many Buddhists are pacifists [i.e. they do not believe that violence is ever justified].

FINDING REFUGE

Buddhism does not set out to make new converts but many people in Western countries have become Buddhists in recent years. They find that the religion answers many of the questions that they are asking. The ceremony by which they become a Buddhist is very simple and is called 'Going for refuge'. This means that the person is committed to:

- Go to the Buddha for refuge – to take him as their example in everything.

- Go to the **Dharma** [the teachings of Buddhism] for refuge – to follow those teachings faithfully.

- Go to the sangha for refuge – to join a Buddhist community to find help and inspiration.

These are called the **Three Refuges** or **Three Jewels** of Buddhism.

JOINING THE SANGHA

In the time of the Buddha, the sangha meant the whole Buddhist community. Now, in Mahayana Buddhism, it means the community of monks and nuns. This is the community in which all Buddhists join to help one another on their spiritual journey.

As we shall see in Unit 13, there are no set days on which Buddhists go to the **monastery** or temple to take part in worship. Many Buddhists, however, do worship on days of the new moon or the full moon [called **Uposatha days**], when they take gifts of food and clothing to the monks and take part in their meditation. The monks believe that the goods they receive are in return for the teaching that they give to ordinary Buddhists.

OVER TO **YOU** ▶▶▶

1 What are the Three Refuges and why do you think they are often called the Three Jewels.
2 What are the Five Precepts?

TAKE TIME TO THINK

Look carefully at Extract A with your partner. There are five statements here where the second half of the sentence appears to contradict the first half. Take two of these statements and try to work out what they are saying. Report your thoughts back to your class.

IN THE WORLD

During the last decade or two, the teachings of Buddhism have become more widely accepted even by those people who are not Buddhists. Among the most important of these are caring for the environment and treating the world as a resource to be cherished and protected. These concerns mean that Buddhists are able to work closely with all non-violent groups in society, whether they are Buddhist or not.

WHAT BUDDHISM IS ABOUT

One saying is often repeated at Buddhist festivals and this sums up what the religion is all about:

A   "*Close your eyes and you will see clearly,*
Cease to listen and you will hear the truth,
Be silent and your heart will sing,
Be gentle and you will need no strength,
Be patient and you will achieve all things."

Meditation is a very important way for Buddhists to understand and follow the teachings of the Buddha.

THE THREE SIGNS OF BEING

You will find out

- The Three Signs of Being.
- About anicca.
- About anatta.
- About dukkha.

In the glossary

Anatta

Anicca

Buddha

Dukkha

Eight-Fold Path

Four Noble Truths

Nibbana

Skandha

The Olympic flame is transferred from one torch to another and yet it remains the same flame.

The Buddha himself said:

A *"The best of paths is the path of eight; the best of truths the four sayings; the best of states, freedom from passions; the best of men, the one who sees. This is the path, there is no other that leads to Visions. Whoever goes on this path travels to the end of sorrow."*

Dhammapada 20.273-6

For most Buddhist believers, the teaching of the Buddha can be summed up in three parts:

- The Three Signs of Being.
- The Four Noble Truths [Unit 7].
- The Noble Eight-Fold Path [Unit 8].

Taken together, Buddhists believe that these teachings show human beings the best way to live their lives.

THE THREE SIGNS OF BEING

These are sometimes called the Three Universal Truths and are the foundation of all human existence:

Anicca

This word means 'impermanence' – everything in the world is constantly changing and so nothing lasts forever. Not even human existence is permanent. Many people find this idea very disturbing but it is important, as a Buddhist, to hold on to the idea that a person's personality constantly changes and grows. It is this constantly changing personality that is our true 'self'.

The photograph helps us to understand this. The Olympic Flame is transferred from person to person on its journey to the stadium. Each flame, apart from the first, is lit by the one that has gone before. It is the same flame that proceeds from person to person.

Anatta

This idea follows on from anicca. There is no unchangeable 'soul' or 'self' in everyone. Yet there is a 'person' and the person is made up of five parts [called '**skandhas**']. They are:

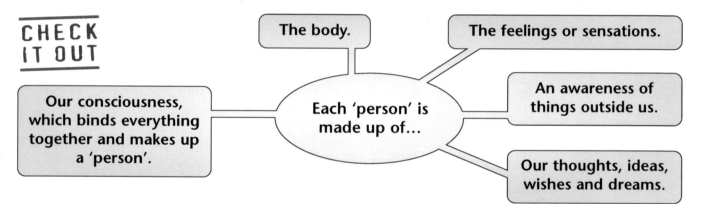

CHECK
IT OUT

Our consciousness, which binds everything together and makes up a 'person'.

The body.

The feelings or sensations.

Each 'person' is made up of...

An awareness of things outside us.

Our thoughts, ideas, wishes and dreams.

When we die, all of these things fall apart and make up another person. It is only when nibbana is finally reached that the skandhas are dispersed, since there is no further use for them.

Dukkha

In this life, everything changes. However wonderful life might be now, change will inevitably lead to suffering. This belief [dukkha] is one of the Four Noble Truths and we will find out more about this in Unit 7.

OVER TO **YOU** ▶▶

1 What is anicca?
2 What is anatta?
3 What happens when a person reaches nibbana?

TAKE TIME TO THINK

Someone once asked the Buddha whether existence was an illusion. He kept quiet and offered no answer. When a disciple asked him afterwards why he had said nothing, the Buddha replied:

"If I had answered that anything is eternal [lasts forever] it would have been misunderstood. If I had said that nothing exists that, too, would have been misunderstood."

After reading the answer, can you begin to explain why the Buddha offered no answer to the original question?

THE FOUR NOBLE TRUTHS

You will find out

- The Four Noble Truths of Buddhism.

In the glossary

Buddha

Dukkha

Enlightenment

Four Noble Truths

Middle Way

Siddhartha Gautama

Buddha explained to his monks just what suffering is:

A *"This is the Noble Truth of Suffering; death is suffering; presence of objects we hate is suffering; separation from others we love is suffering; not to obtain what we desire is suffering. Briefly, the five-fold clinging to existence is suffering. All existence is dukkha [suffering]."*

The Four Noble Truths are the insights that the Buddha received while he sat under the bodhi tree. Buddhists say that these Truths are the most important part of his teaching, since they teach about suffering and how it can be overcome. The Buddha taught that, when people accept them, then they will be able to change their lives forever.

The Buddha taught that suffering is everywhere and all people suffer.

THE FIRST NOBLE TRUTH –
SUFFERING HAPPENS EVERYWHERE, ALL THE TIME

It was only when Siddhartha Gautama saw an old man, a sick man and a dead man that he began to understand the true nature of suffering. He realised that nothing lasts forever and even the happiest moments in life vanish like vapour into the air. Every life, from birth, has something wrong with it.

TAKE TIME TO THINK

Think of three examples of suffering in the modern world which help you to understand the Buddha's explanation of what suffering is in Extract A.

THE SECOND NOBLE TRUTH – SUFFERING IS CAUSED BY SELFISHNESS

Buddhists believe that everyone is born selfish. We are always more concerned with our own welfare than the welfare of others. We desire people, things and a continued existence in our pursuit of happiness. Even if our desire is temporarily satisfied, it returns to control us – and bring suffering.

THE THIRD NOBLE TRUTH – THERE CAN BE RELEASE FROM SUFFERING

This is the Buddha's remedy for the ills of this world. A person must begin by eliminating all selfish desires and the craving for attachment to this world. To do this, he or she must avoid going to one of two extremes – to living a life of poverty or living a life of luxury. The way to happiness lies in between the two.

THE FOURTH NOBLE TRUTH – TO FOLLOW THE MIDDLE PATH

Speaking to his monks, the Buddha told them:

> B   *"There are two extremes that should not be practised. And what are these two? That devoted to passions and luxury – which is low, unworthy, vulgar and useless; and that devoted to self-mortification, which is painful, unworthy and useless. By avoiding these two extremes, the Perfect One [the Buddha] has gained the enlightenment."*

The Buddha provided his followers with several pictures to help them understand the Middle Way. He spoke of it being like:

CHECK IT OUT

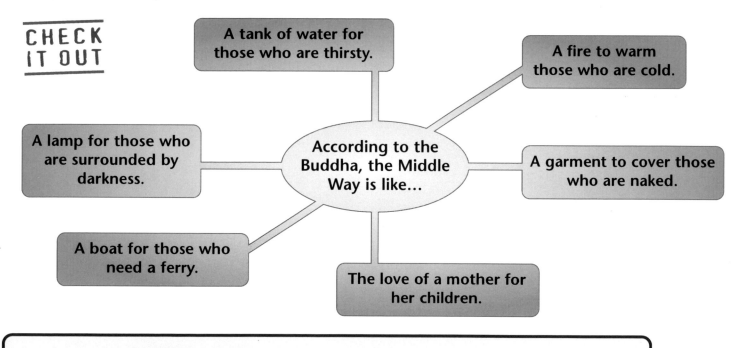

A tank of water for those who are thirsty.

A fire to warm those who are cold.

A lamp for those who are surrounded by darkness.

According to the Buddha, the Middle Way is like...

A garment to cover those who are naked.

A boat for those who need a ferry.

The love of a mother for her children.

OVER TO YOU ▶▶▶

Read Extract B carefully:

1 What two extremes are monks told to avoid in their search for enlightenment?
2 What is the Middle Way and what can it lead to?
3 Why do you think that Buddhism has been called 'the Balanced Way'? Do you think that this means sitting on the fence and not being committed to anything?
4 How did the Buddha himself achieve enlightenment?

THE EIGHT-FOLD PATH

You will find out

- About the Noble Eight-Fold Path.

In the glossary

Buddha

Dukkha

Eight-Fold Path

Middle Way

Nibbana

The Buddha, then, encouraged his followers to find the Middle Way between luxury and poverty to reach nibbana. There are eight clear steps to do this and all of them need to be acted on at the same time. Only then will a believer have the blueprint to conquer greed and hatred, which are the root causes of suffering.

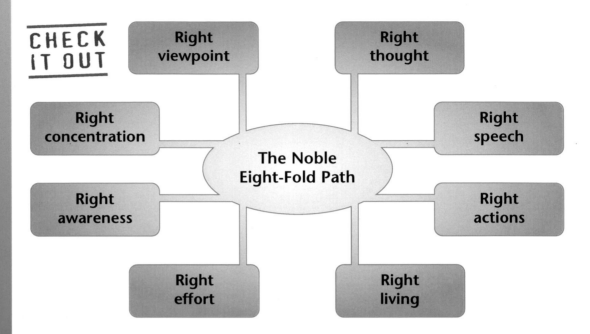

CHECK IT OUT

Right viewpoint · Right thought · Right speech · Right actions · Right living · Right effort · Right awareness · Right concentration · **The Noble Eight-Fold Path**

RIGHT VIEWPOINT

Unless a person looks at life in the right way, they will never achieve nibbana. To do this, they must accept the basic beliefs of Buddhism and begin by accepting that all life is dukkha [suffering/unsatisfactory].

RIGHT THOUGHT

A person's mind is very powerful and it needs to be used in the right way. Having loving thoughts to all living creatures, even the most humble, leads a person to be caring and unselfish. It prevents them from concentrating on themselves alone.

RIGHT SPEECH

The words that come out of a person's mouth not only show their true character but also have the power to hurt and wound others. Telling lies and swearing should be avoided. Instead, a person's speech should be pure, kind and helpful.

RIGHT ACTIONS

Right actions include avoiding killing any living being, not stealing and not being dishonest. For almost all Buddhists, this means not killing animals for food – they are vegetarian. It also means abstaining from those things that lessen self-control, such as drinking alcohol.

Showing love in everyday life is an important part of following the Noble Eight-Fold Path.

RIGHT LIVING

Someone who wants to follow the Buddha's teachings should be careful about the job that they do. It should be useful to the community and avoid anything that harms others.

RIGHT EFFORT

All bad thoughts should be banished from the mind. Bad thoughts lead to bad actions.

RIGHT MINDFULNESS

All those seeking to follow the Middle Way should be aware of the needs of others. As this is not the natural thing to do, it requires great self-control.

RIGHT CONCENTRATION

Training the mind to concentrate properly comes about by meditation. The mind that can concentrate becomes calm, collected and at peace with itself. Nothing, then, can distract the person from following the Middle Way.

OVER TO YOU ▶▶▶

1 What do you think the word 'right' means in the Noble Eight-Fold Path?

2 The Buddha's teaching about right living includes working hard but not harming others. What sort of jobs do you think a Buddhist might be advised to avoid?

3 Many people use meditation, although not all of them, by any means, are Buddhists. What do you think they might gain from meditation?

TAKE TIME TO THINK

Do you think it is easy for someone to follow the Noble Eight-Fold Path? Describe the things in your life that would have to change if you were to follow the Noble Eight-Fold Path.

THE THREE REFUGES

Buddhists rely for help and teaching on the Three Refuges, also called the Three Jewels. They express this in a particular form of words, the repetition of which is called 'taking refuge'. The Three Refuges are used when someone wants to become a Buddhist and at the beginning of most Buddhist activities.

The Three Refuges are:

A *"I go the Buddha for refuge.*
I go to the Dharma [the teaching of the Buddha] for refuge.
I go to the sangha [the Buddhist community] for refuge."

These are the three precious and helpful foundations of Buddhist belief and worship.

Monks and laypeople find refuge in the monastic community, which is at the heart of Buddhism.

I GO TO THE BUDDHA FOR REFUGE

Buddhists teach that the true nature and destiny of all human beings is the state of enlightenment – nibbana. This can also be called the Buddha Nature. It lies like a seed within each human being and can be symbolised by the image of a full moon, partly or totally hidden behind clouds.

The different Buddhist practices, and especially meditation, are all designed to help people to realise their full potential as human beings. They are taking refuge in the Buddha each time they spend time meditating and worshipping. The more they do this, the more they realise that they share the Buddha Nature with all other beings.

I GO TO THE DHARMA FOR REFUGE

The Dharma refers to the truth about the way things are – the law of life. It is what the Buddha discovered at his enlightenment and what he later taught people. It is summed up in the Four Noble Truths and the Eight-Fold Path.

I GO TO THE SANGHA FOR REFUGE

The sangha is the whole Buddhist community and this plays a very large part in the growth and development of the awareness of the truth that is found in Buddhism. Belonging to this community means becoming a part of the Buddhist family – past and present.

This community is made up of four groups of people:

CHECK IT OUT

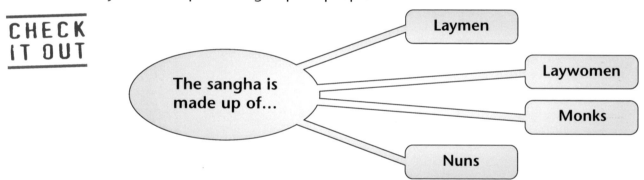

The sangha is made up of...
- Laymen
- Laywomen
- Monks
- Nuns

Members of these groups can also be called 'the sons and daughters of the Buddha'. Through belonging to this community, Buddhists learn to put aside everything that would separate them from others by purifying their hearts of greed, ignorance and hatred. It then becomes possible to share with others the loving kindness and compassion that are to be found at the heart of Buddhism.

The sangha depends on the laypeople for gifts of food, clothing and shelter. In return, its members preserve meditation practices and study of the holy texts as well as teaching the Dharma to ordinary Buddhists.

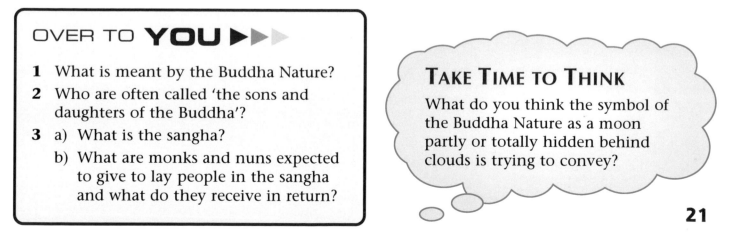

OVER TO YOU ▶▶▶

1 What is meant by the Buddha Nature?
2 Who are often called 'the sons and daughters of the Buddha'?
3 a) What is the sangha?
   b) What are monks and nuns expected to give to lay people in the sangha and what do they receive in return?

TAKE TIME TO THINK

What do you think the symbol of the Buddha Nature as a moon partly or totally hidden behind clouds is trying to convey?

The **Ten Precepts** are the promises, or vows, that Buddhists make. Monks follow all ten of the promises while laypeople are expected to keep the first five. They also keep the following four when they are on meditation retreats and during certain religious festivals.

All of the precepts are based on certain Buddhist beliefs about life and the universe:

PRECEPT 1: TO REFRAIN FROM HARMING ANY LIVING THING

This belief, taken over from Hinduism, is called **ahimsa**. An action is wrong if the intention behind it is wrong. Non-harming starts in the heart and Buddhists are encouraged to cultivate 'loving kindness' for this reason.

PRECEPT 2: TO REFRAIN FROM TAKING WHAT IS NOT GIVEN

All lay Buddhists must conduct their personal and business life in a blameless way. To do otherwise is to defraud other people. The person who defrauds loses their chance of enjoying happiness. A monk must not take anything that does not belong to him – all that he has must be given.

PRECEPT 3: TO REFRAIN FROM A MISUSE OF THE SENSES

All Buddhists must live a chaste life and not misuse their sexuality. Adultery and promiscuity are wrong.

PRECEPT 4: TO REFRAIN FROM WRONG SPEECH

Anyone who lies or withholds the truth goes against the teaching of the Buddha. To do this destroys any hope that a person may have of enjoying personal happiness.

PRECEPT 5: TO REFRAIN FROM TAKING INTOXICANTS

Intoxicants, such as alcohol or unnecessary drugs, only cloud the mind. If the mind is blurred, the person cannot lead any kind of thoughtful life – and that is essential for happiness.

PRECEPT 6: TO REFRAIN FROM EATING AT TIMES OTHER THAN THOSE WHICH ARE LAID DOWN

The times of the day when monks are allowed to eat are laid down by their monastic routine. Monks do not eat after twelve noon each day.

PRECEPT 7: TO REFRAIN FROM DANCING, SINGING AND MUSIC

These activities are considered to be unseemly for monks.

Many Buddhists use prayer wheels to help them to follow the Ten Precepts.

PRECEPT 8: TO REFRAIN FROM USING GARLANDS, PERFUMES AND DEODORANTS

Monks must spend no time trying to beautify their person.

PRECEPT 9: TO REFRAIN FROM USING HIGH AND LUXURIOUS BEDS

These are part of the lifestyle that monks turn their back on when they follow the Middle Way.

PRECEPT 10: TO REFRAIN FROM ACCEPTING GOLD OR SILVER

These two gifts signify the life of luxury that the true Buddhist monk and nun have turned their backs on.

To underline the importance of not carrying 'extra baggage' on their journey through life, the Buddha told his followers a **parable**:

A   "*I will teach you the parable of the raft. Listen to it and pay careful attention. It is like a man who as he is going on a journey should see a great stretch of water, this bank with dangers and fears, the farther bank secure and without fears, but there may be neither a boat for crossing over, nor a bridge across for going from the not-beyond to the beyond. It occurs to him that in order to cross over from the perils of this bank to the security of the other bank he should fashion a raft out of grass and sticks, branches and foliage so that he can cross over to the beyond in safety.*"

OVER TO **YOU** ▶▶▶

Look at the parable in Extract A carefully.

1 What is a parable?
2 What do you think the Buddha wanted to convey by the journey that this man took and the great stretch of water that he went across?
3 What do you think the raft stands for?
4 What is the significance of the fact that the raft is made out of ordinary things that need to be bound together to have any strength.

TAKE TIME TO THINK

In the parable of the raft, what do you think the safe bank in the distance symbolises?

NATURAL LAWS

Everyone knows that we all have to live our lives according to certain basic laws or rules. These laws govern the whole of nature. Here are two examples:

- What happens when you throw any object in the air? It falls back to Earth. Why? It is drawn irresistibly towards the centre of the Earth by gravity.

- What happens when someone hits someone else in the eye? They soon discover that there is an opposite reaction to every action. Any force moving in one direction can be met by another object moving in the opposite direction. The result can be very painful!

These two examples are called 'natural laws'. Buddhists believe that there is another natural law that affects all of us – the law of **karma**.

THE LAW OF KARMA

Put quite simply, the law of karma teaches that everything that we say, do or think will have some future effect upon us. Put it another way – everything that happens to us has the effect of causing something else to happen to us in the future.

As everyone knows, we can do good or bad things. So:

- If we do or think a good action or thought then good or positive things will happen to us in the future as a direct result.

But:

- If we do or think bad things then bad things will happen to us in the future.

This means that, if you wonder why something good has happened to you in this life, then the clue is to be found in a past life. If something bad happens in your present life, then the reason is to be found in the past. If you want to influence your life in a good way in the future, then be careful how you are living your life now.

OVER TO YOU ▶▶▶

1 Here is a game you can play with the whole class. It begins with the first person thinking of a real-life situation. The next person thinks of something that could happen as a result of that situation. The third person thinks of something that could happen as a result of the second situation and so on. Compare the first situation with the last. What does the game teach you?

2 Imagine that you are a Buddhist. How do you think your belief in karma might affect the way that you live?

SAMSARA

Buddhists believe, then, that everything that happens to them now is the result of something they have done in the past. Everything they do now is the cause of something that will happen to them in the future. The whole of their life is a vast web of causes and effects.

As we shall see in Unit 25, Buddhists believe that the law of karma continues after we die – but in another body. In this way, what goes around always comes around – it is a basic law of nature:

As we shall see in Unit 25,

CHECK IT OUT

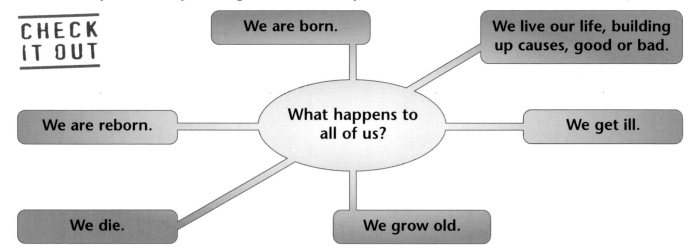

We are born.

We live our life, building up causes, good or bad.

What happens to all of us?

We are reborn.

We get ill.

We die.

We grow old.

Life goes round and round in the same endless circle. Birth, old age, death and rebirth are repeated for all of us many times. Through each rebirth, we are building an endless stream of causes, good or bad, which have an endless number of effects.

This cycle of existence is called **samsara**. We are living in a world of impermanence and suffering and only the teaching of the Buddha can show us the way to escape from it.

TAKE TIME TO THINK

Buddhists believe that everything we do is a cause, which will have a future effect. What do you think a Buddhist might believe the effect of dying to be?

THE WHEEL OF LIFE

You will find out

- About the Wheel of Life.

- The significance of the circles in the Wheel of Life.

In the glossary

Buddha

Enlightenment

Samsara

The Wheel of Life is the traditional Buddhist way of showing the cycle from birth through to death – and then rebirth.

In Unit 11, you were introduced to the Buddhist belief in samsara. The Wheel of Life is the name given to a particular kind of picture, which illustrates the way that Buddhists understand samsara. You can find an example of this picture above.

THE WHEEL OF LIFE

As you can see from the picture, there are four circles in the Wheel of Life:

Circle A

In this circle, there are three animals – the cockerel symbolising desire, the snake as a symbol of hatred and the pig standing for ignorance. These are the three fires, or root evils, which stand in the way of everyone who wishes to reach enlightenment. As such, they need to be overcome.

Circle B

Here we have figures which are both rising and falling to show that people can make progress, or go backwards, in their search for enlightenment.

Circle C

At the top of this circle are people who are carefree as they follow their own interests. This is the realm of the gods. Next come the power seekers who are always at war. They are portrayed as jealous, warring gods. This is followed by the realm of the animals, who live according to their basic instincts. At the bottom are the hell realms, where beings are in constant torment. Finally, the realm of human beings, who understand the reality and accept the need for non-attachment. These people are likely to attain enlightenment.

Circle D

Around the edge of the wheel are twelve pictures, which represent the cycle of causes and effects that lead from birth to sickness, to old age and death and then back to rebirth.

The whole circle is held in the grip of a fierce demon, called Yama, who personifies impermanence, change and death. The demon represents the suffering that every human being has to endure.

IS THERE ANY HOPE?

There is hope in the rather depressing picture that the Wheel of Life paints. Inside each of the life-state segments there is a Buddha. This shows that anyone, whatever they are like, can become enlightened and happy.

Some Buddhists use the Wheel of Life as a basis for their own meditations. It gives them the opportunity to reflect on their own life and its progress towards enlightenment.

OVER TO **YOU** ▶▶▶

The Wheel of Life represents the main moods through which all of us pass. Among the moods represented are depression, greed and anger.

1 Write down six moods, both good and bad, that you sometimes experience.
2 Draw a bar graph of your own moods to show those that are very common – and those that are less common.
3 Compare your graph with that of your partner. Are they similar or not? What conclusion do you draw from this?

TAKE TIME TO THINK

Buddhism teaches that all moods have a good [positive] side and a bad [negative] side. Take three of the moods that you included in your bar graph and explain what you think the good and bad sides of them might be.

Buddhists can worship on their own or with other Buddhists. There is no special day of the week for Buddhists to worship, although the days before the new, full and half moon are particularly important. Many Buddhists believe that:

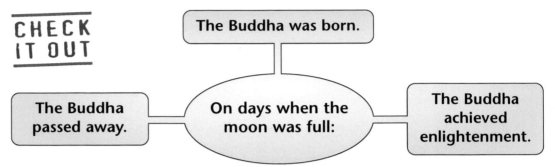

CHECK IT OUT

The Buddha was born.

The Buddha passed away.

On days when the moon was full:

The Buddha achieved enlightenment.

SHRINES

Buddhist worship usually takes place in front of a shrine. A shrine is a special place thought to be holy because of what it holds. Buddhist shrines always hold:

- An image of the Buddha – called a **rupa**.
- Holders for incense, a spice which has a strong, sweet smell as it burns.
- Flowers and candles.
- Places where offerings of fruit and flowers can be left.

A Buddhist temple will have its own shrine room. So, too, will many Buddhist homes.

Water is an important offering made by Buddhists.

Fruit is another important offering made in front of the statue of the Buddha.

GROUP WORSHIP

When Buddhists arrive for worship in a **vihara** or monastery, they remove their shoes. This is a mark of respect, as it is in many religions. Worshippers sit on the floor and it shows a lack of respect to point their feet towards the image of the Buddha.

When Buddhists pass in front of the image, they put their hands together and nod their head. They make offerings of fruit, flowers and light [by lighting a candle], before following the monks as they lead the worship. You can find a prayer that often accompanies the making of an offering in Extract A:

A *"I make the offering to the Buddha with these flowers and through this merit may there be release. Even as the flowers must fade so my body goes toward destruction."*

There are readings from the Buddhist holy books and the monk may give a talk. At the close of the act of worship, the people may stay behind and drink tea together.

TAKE TIME TO THINK

Why do you think that flowers are thought to be a suitable offering to make and what do they remind the worshipper about?

INDIVIDUAL WORSHIP

Most Buddhists also conduct personal acts of worship before their own home shrine. During this, they meditate and read sections from the holy books. They often burn incense and offer gifts of flowers and food in front of the Buddha's image. They may also light candles.

As we have already seen, Theravada Buddhists do not pray but Mahayana Buddhists may offer up prayers to the bodhisattvas for their help.

OVER TO **YOU** ▶▶▶

Incense is frequently offered up before the Buddha. This offering is accompanied by the words:

B *"To him of fragrant body and face, fragrant with infinite values. To the Buddha I make offering with fragrant incense."*

1 What does the word 'fragrant' mean?
2 With what is the Buddha said to be fragrant?

You will find out

- The meaning of the Buddhist rupa.
- The symbolic importance of the rupa.
- The value of mandalas.

In the glossary

Buddha

Eight-Fold Path

Four Noble Truths

Rupa

Buddhist teaching includes many things that are difficult to understand. To help his followers, the Buddha used symbols to make them easier to understand. Flowers, for example, are often used as offerings at Buddhist shrines because they quickly wither and die. This powerfully illustrates the Buddhist belief that nothing, including life itself, lasts for ever.

THE RUPA

Buddhists believe that the teaching of the Buddha is the only guide that they need for life. This is why nearly all Buddhists have a statue of the Buddha [called a rupa] in their home. This is a constant reminder of those teachings which are summed up in Extract A:

A *"The best of paths is the path of the eight [Noble Eight-Fold Path]; the best of truths the four sayings [the Four Noble Truths]. The best of states, freedom from passion. The best of men, the one who sees. This is the path, there is no other that leads to visitations. Whoever goes along this path travels to the end of sorrow."*

Dhammapada 20.273-6

Each rupa shows the Buddha in one of three different positions – standing, sitting or lying down. His hands are shown in different positions to indicate different aspects of his teaching. When the rupa is sitting down, he is often in the lotus position, meditating. If he is teaching, he is usually sitting with one hand raised.

Each rupa shows one or many of 32 symbols indicating that the Buddha was not an ordinary human being. Here are four of those symbols:

- There is a bump on the top of his head to show he had special gifts.
- He has a round mark on his forehead, called 'the third eye'. This shows that he could 'see' things that other human beings could not.
- He has long ear lobes to show that he comes from an important family.
- His hair is tightly curled, showing that he was a holy man.

THE MANDALA

A mandala is a specially designed pattern made up of circles, triangles and squares. The Wheel of the Law, a wheel made up of eight spokes to show the Noble Eight-Fold Path, is a mandala. Mandalas are symbols to illustrate Buddhist beliefs and are often used to help people in their meditation.

OVER TO YOU ▶▶▶

1 a) What is a rupa?
   b) Why are you likely to see a rupa if you enter the home of a Buddhist?
2 According to Extract A, what is the best of paths and what is the best of truths?
3 How do Buddhists know that the statue of the Buddha is special?

There are many signs that the statue of the Buddha is special.

MONASTERIES AND STUPAS

In Unit 13, you were introduced to shrines as important places of Buddhist worship. Here you will find out about two other places of worship.

MONASTERIES

Ever since the time of the Buddha's enlightenment, there have been men and women prepared to give up everything to find the meaning of life. These people are members of the monastic sangha [called **bhikkhus**] – the community of Buddhist monks. They are the living link with the Buddha and his teaching. They live together in monasteries.

Anyone entering a Buddhist monastery has to go through a trial period before being ordained. The demands placed upon them are virtually the same as those demanded of a monk in the Buddha's lifetime:

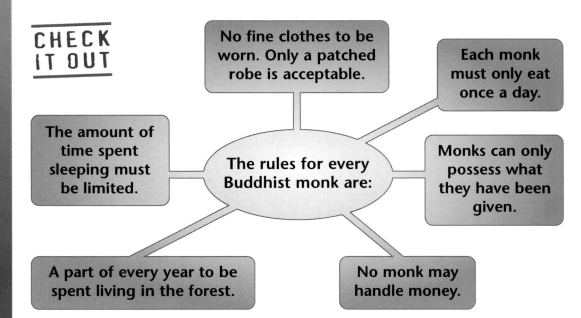

CHECK IT OUT

The rules for every Buddhist monk are:

- No fine clothes to be worn. Only a patched robe is acceptable.
- Each monk must only eat once a day.
- Monks can only possess what they have been given.
- No monk may handle money.
- A part of every year to be spent living in the forest.
- The amount of time spent sleeping must be limited.

There are 227 rules governing the everyday conduct of the monk. All of their basic needs are provided by the wider Buddhist community. In return, the monks teach the people freely about the Buddhist way of life. Ordinary people go to the monastery to worship and study, guided by the monks. Many children also go to their local monastery to be taught to read and write by the monks.

MONASTERY GARDENS

Gardens play an important part in several religions. Monasteries almost always have gardens and these offer relief to the monks from the burning rays of the sun. In this way, they help to create a calm and peaceful atmosphere. The plants in the garden of a monastery are spiritually important. The Buddha taught his disciples that nothing lasts forever – everything is impermanent. Plants demonstrate the truth of this. They grow but soon die.

A stupa in India.

STUPAS

A **stupa** is a building that has a rounded top, like a hill. After the Buddha died, his body was cremated and his ashes were taken to eight different places which had been important during his lifetime. Stupas were then built where the ashes were buried.

Another two stupas were built:
- Over the place where his body had been burned.
- Over the place where the urn that held his ashes had been buried.

Ten stupas were built in all, although others were later erected to commemorate great teachers or holy men.

TAKE TIME TO THINK

Why do you think that monks are only allowed to wear a patched robe and are not allowed to handle money?

OVER TO **YOU** ▶▶▶

1 Imagine that you want to become a Buddhist monk or nun. Look at the six rules that you would have to obey. Place them in order, ranging from the most difficult to keep to the easiest. Compare your order with that of your partner. Do you largely agree or not?

2 Explain the link between the monks and the lay Buddhists. Why do they need each other?

3 a) What is a stupa?
   b) Where have stupas been built in the past?
   c) Describe what a stupa looks like from the photograph in this unit.

33

THE LIFE OF A BUDDHIST MONK

In the Theravada tradition of Buddhism, there are two stages through which monks and nuns seeking ordination must pass:

- As a 'novice' [beginner], the monk or nun follows the Ten Precepts as we saw in Unit 10.
- At the age of 20, the monk or nun can pass on to 'higher ordination'.

THE ROBE AND THE ALMS BOWL

The outward symbol of the devotion of the monk to the teachings of the Buddha is the saffron robe that he always wears. This is the traditional colour worn in India by those who have turned their backs on the world in search of spiritual salvation.

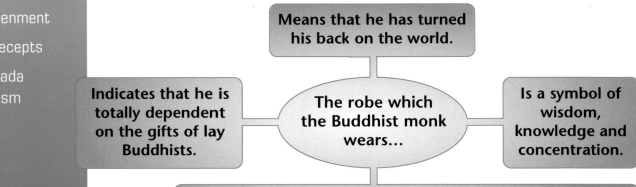

Means that he has turned his back on the world.

Indicates that he is totally dependent on the gifts of lay Buddhists.

The robe which the Buddhist monk wears...

Is a symbol of wisdom, knowledge and concentration.

Symbolises the fact that the monk has discovered how to be released from the desire that causes all suffering.

Monks are on the street every day in Buddhist countries to receive offerings from the people.

Buddhists believe that the presence of monks in their community is very important.

In Theravada countries, it is very common to see saffron-robed monks carrying their alms bowls to collect the gifts of the faithful. They do so in silence because they are not allowed to ask people for their gifts. Ordinary Buddhists must be ready to offer food since this provides them with the opportunity of earning merit.

EVERYDAY LIFE

Buddhist monks are only allowed to eat one main meal a day. This leaves them free for the rest of the day to devote themselves to meditation, study, teaching the laity and carrying out practical work. In all this, they have two main responsibilities:

- They must meditate so that their own enlightenment is brought nearer. In many Buddhist traditions, meditation is said to be the main work of the monk.
- They must preserve the teachings of the Buddha faithfully and pass them on to the people, to help lead them to enlightenment.

This does not mean that all Buddhist monks live under the same conditions. In some monastic communities, situated in remote places, the lifestyle is very simple and meditation is given the highest priority. In other communities, priests spend most of their time looking after the local shrine. Yet other priests spend most of their time writing books.

Although most Buddhist monks and nuns live in settled communities, there is a tradition of trying to shake off attachment to this world by simply walking through the countryside for weeks or even years [A].

A "*When the walk came to an end, 13 mornings after leaving, the practice-path that it symbolises continued; the monastic life is about non-abiding, it is a giving up of personal possessions, desires, concerns and opinions. You listen and live close to the heart of life, and the only refuge from the rawness of nature is to do good and be mindful. Sometimes that seems to leave you completely alone with nothing to hold on to, but the path evokes a compassion in us that fills the heart and a respect for our way of life that gives us many friends.*"

Buddhist monk after taking walk

TAKE TIME TO THINK

Why do you think that a Buddhist monk or nun is considered to be a very important part of the Buddhist community?

OVER TO YOU ▶▶▶

Look at the monk's description of his 'spiritual walk'.

1 What do you think he meant when he said "The practice-path that it symbolises continued..."?

2 What indication is there in this extract that the path chosen by a Buddhist monk is not an easy one?

3 When the going appears to be hard, what does the monk take refuge in?

You will find out

- The origins of the Dechen Community.
- The different levels on which instruction is given to those who visit the Dechen Community.
- The two main teachers in the Dechen Community.

In the glossary

Dharma

Enlightenment

Meditation

Reincarnation

Lama Jampa Thaye, dharma regent of Karma Thinley Rinpoche.

Karma Thinley Rinpoche, founder of the Dechen Community.

Dechen seal, designed by Karma Thinley Rinpoche.

BEGINNINGS

In 1988, Karma Thinley Rinpoche bestowed the name 'Dechen' on many teaching groups and centres that represented Tibetan Buddhism in the UK and Europe. These groups had been established in his name by his principal disciple, Lama Jampa Thaye.

The word 'dechen' is the Tibetan for 'great bliss' and had recently come to Rinpoche in a dream, where he had composed a poem in which the first line was 'Great bliss is the antidote to laziness'.

People are believed to experience great bliss, 'dechen', when they master the spiritual practices that are taught at these spiritual centres. The ultimate goal of such spiritual practices is complete enlightenment.

THE DECHEN COMMUNITY

The Dechen Community offers instruction and teaching on three different levels:

Level 1: This is the elementary level at which newcomers [beginners] are taught the basics about meditation and Buddhist teachings from students who have reached a more advanced level.

Level 2: Once a beginner has some knowledge about meditation and how it can help them, they are taken on to the next level. For this, they attend lectures and practical sessions on more advanced meditation practices and topics.

Level 3: At this level, students receive personal instruction from Lama Jampa Thaye on the most advanced meditation practices of the Tibetan tradition and study the major philosophical texts.

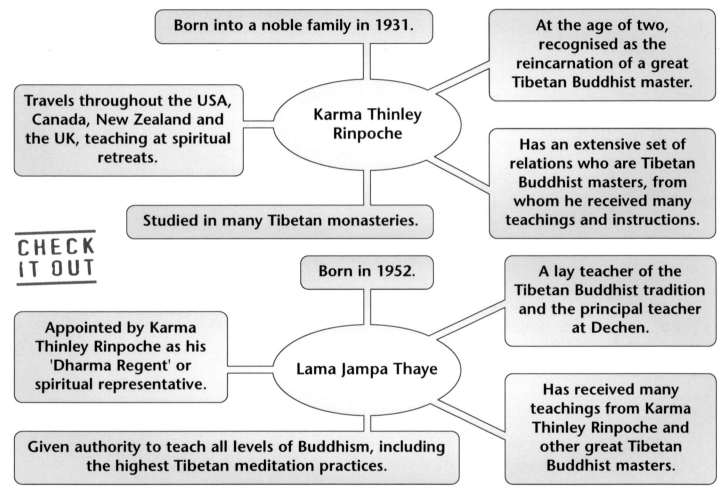

CHECK
IT OUT

Born into a noble family in 1931.

At the age of two, recognised as the reincarnation of a great Tibetan Buddhist master.

Travels throughout the USA, Canada, New Zealand and the UK, teaching at spiritual retreats.

Karma Thinley Rinpoche

Has an extensive set of relations who are Tibetan Buddhist masters, from whom he received many teachings and instructions.

Studied in many Tibetan monasteries.

Born in 1952.

A lay teacher of the Tibetan Buddhist tradition and the principal teacher at Dechen.

Appointed by Karma Thinley Rinpoche as his 'Dharma Regent' or spiritual representative.

Lama Jampa Thaye

Has received many teachings from Karma Thinley Rinpoche and other great Tibetan Buddhist masters.

Given authority to teach all levels of Buddhism, including the highest Tibetan meditation practices.

You can find out much more information about the Dechen Community by visiting www.dechen.org/index.html.

OVER TO **YOU** ▶▶▶

1 Explain why the Dechen Community was given its name.

2 a) What do you understand by the word 'bliss'?

b) What was the time when you experienced the greatest bliss?

c) Was it an experience that you would like to repeat? Explain your answer.

TAKE TIME TO THINK

The Dechen Community exists to help people to learn to meditate. If someone asked you what meditation is, how would you answer them? Why do you think that many people find that meditation helps them in this very busy world? Do you think that it is something that could help you? If so, in what way?

You will find out

- About the Pali Canon of the Buddhist scriptures.
- About the Mahayana scriptures.
- About the hidden scriptures of the Tibetan Buddhists.

In the glossary

Bodhissatva

Buddha

Dharma

Eight-Fold Path

Four Noble Truths

Mahayana Buddhism

Pali Canon

Parable

Sutta Pitaka

Theravada Buddhism

Three Baskets

Tipitaka

In the time of the Buddha, few people could read or write. They had to remember the teachings of the Buddha. To help them, the Buddha used many methods to put over his teaching, including:

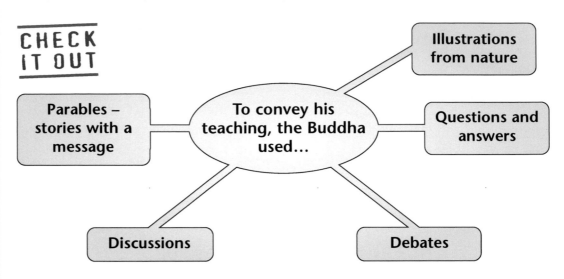

CHECK IT OUT

To convey his teaching, the Buddha used...

- Parables – stories with a message
- Illustrations from nature
- Questions and answers
- Discussions
- Debates

Yet he did not write anything down himself or leave a written record of his teaching. When he died, his disciples, the monks, began to write down all that they could remember of his teaching. This lasted for about 400 years. The material was organised into three main collections:

1. THE PALI CANON

This collection was written in the Pali language and is used by Theravada Buddhists. It is also called the **Tipitaka** or **Three Baskets**. It is called this because these scriptures were first written on leaves that were collected into three baskets:

- The rules by which the monks should live.
- The teachings of the Buddha. This is the most important basket and is called the **Sutta Pitaka**. A 'sutta' is a small piece of teaching. The most important part is the Path of Teaching, which includes the very important Four Noble Truths [see Unit 7] and the Noble Eight-Fold Path [see Unit 8].
- Writings that help to explain some of the Buddha's teachings.

2. THE MAHAYANA BUDDHIST SCRIPTURES

Mahayana Buddhists have their own versions of much of what is written in the Pali Canon, but they have also added other works. It is claimed that these works carry authority because they are the 'Buddha word'. One of these extra works is named after a householder, Vimalakirti, who was thought to be more holy than any of the bodhissatvas.

TWO LANGUAGES

The Buddhist scriptures were written in the two very old languages of Pali and Sanskrit. As they were written in two different languages, many Buddhist words can be written in two different ways.

Here are two examples:
- Sutta can also be spelled sutra.
- Dharma can also be spelled Dhamma.

Traditionally, the Buddhist scriptures were written on any material available.

3. THE HIDDEN SCRIPTURES OF THE TIBETAN BUDDHISTS

Tibetan Buddhists believe that many scriptures were hidden until the community was ready to receive, and understand, their teachings. These 'hidden scriptures' are still being found today. The most widely known of them is called 'The Tibetan Book of the Dead'.

OVER TO YOU ▶▶▶

Here are some questions about the Buddhist holy books. You may need to carry out some research of your own to answer one or two of them:

1 What are the main books of Theravada and Mahayana Buddhism?

2 In which languages are the books of Mahayana and Theravada Buddhism written?

3 Why is the term 'basket' used for the most important Buddhist books?

4 What is the link between a lotus flower and the Buddhist scriptures?

TEACHERS MATTER

You will find out

- Why Buddhists need good teachers on their spiritual journey.

- The line of tradition behind every Buddhist teacher.

In the glossary

Buddha

Enlightenment

Mahayana Buddhism

Nibbana

Sangha

Theravada Buddhism

Teachers are very important for maintaining the purity of the Buddhist religion.

As soon as he was enlightened, the Buddha could have gone to nibbana, but he chose not to. Instead he elected to remain behind on Earth and he spent the next 40 years teaching others how to reach enlightenment. His message to them was about just one thing – how they could understand suffering and bring it to an end in their own lives.

WHY TEACHERS MATTER

The part that teachers play in the tradition of Buddhism is very important. They follow in the footsteps of the Buddha by trying to help others towards the truth. It is certainly impossible for a Buddhist to reach nibbana without a great deal of spiritual help. It is important to:

* Mahayana Buddhists, where the teacher is someone who comes alongside – a friend on the journey.

* Theravada Buddhists, who believe that their spiritual teachers are elders – those who know more and have much more experience in the work of guiding others.

In the form of Mahayana Buddhism that is found in Tibet, the teachers are called lamas. The most well known teacher in Tibetan Buddhism is the Dalai Lama and we will look at his importance as a Buddhist teacher in Unit 20.

GOOD SPIRITUAL TEACHERS

Buddhist spiritual teachers belong to a long line of tradition of which they are a part. Buddhists often say that, if they are going to climb a high mountain and reach nibbana, then they need to be instructed by someone who has climbed the mountain already. For Buddhist teachers, this means two things:

* The teacher must already have kept the promises or vows of their religious tradition.

* The teacher must have had a genuine experience of the deep meaning of their spiritual tradition.

In the Tibetan Buddhist tradition, something else is also very important. Each teacher inherits a long chain of tradition going way back into history. This line is unbroken and is passed on from one teacher to another. The teacher, in turn, passes on the tradition through his own students and so it is maintained. Tibetan Buddhists believe that this line of tradition is very important since it guarantees that the teaching is kept pure.

This is the reason why the sangha is very important in Buddhist tradition. The community of monks looked after the teachings of the Buddha in the years following his death and they continue to do the same today.

OVER TO YOU ▶▶▶

1 How do you look on your teachers? Do you look on them as older friends? Are they people that you look up to because they have had more experience – and know more about life? Think of three words that most accurately describe the attitudes that you have towards them.

2 List eight characteristics on a spider diagram to describe the characteristics of a perfect teacher for you.

3 What do you think might make a good teacher who is able to help a Buddhist make progress on their spiritual journey?

TAKE TIME TO THINK

After he was enlightened, the Buddha had the opportunity to leave this world and enter nibbana. The same opportunity is given to everyone who reaches enlightenment. The Buddha decided to stay behind on Earth to teach others how to reach nibbana. Why do you think he did this?

THE DALAI LAMA

In the glossary

Buddha

FINDING THE DALAI LAMA

Tenzin Gyatso was born into a peasant family in Takser, in Tibet's Amdo province, in 1935. Two years later, a party of Buddhist monks set out to choose a new spiritual leader as the previous Dalai Lama had been dead four years. For centuries, the Dalai Lamas had been the spiritual and political leaders of Tibet. To Tibetan Buddhists, they were living Buddhas.

They knew that they had found their new spiritual leader when they encountered a two year old boy called Tenzin Gyatso. The party left the boy but promised to return soon. They did so and soon became convinced that the child was the 14th Dalai Lama. He was enthroned in 1940 but he ruled through an older adviser until 1950, when he was 15 years old. The child was given a normal Buddhist education but a change of government in nearby China changed the course of his life.

THE DALAI LAMA AND THE CHINESE

In 1950, the Chinese invaded Tibet. They claimed that they were trying to liberate the Tibetans from the clutches of Western countries such as the USA. The Tibetan army was easily overcome. In 1959, the Dalai Lama was forced to leave Tibet after 10,000 of his fellow countrymen were slaughtered.

The Dalai Lama went into exile. He settled with other Tibetan refugees in Dharamsala, in the Punjab in India. There he set up an alternative government and sought to keep alive many aspects of Tibetan culture and the Buddhist religion.

Since then, as many as 1 million Tibetans, out of a total population of some 5 million, have been killed. In addition, almost 10,000 religious buildings and temples have been destroyed. Many thousands of Chinese have settled in Tibet, making the native Tibetans a minority in their own country.

THE DALAI LAMA TODAY

The Dalai Lama, now well into his seventies, is a highly revered figure in his homeland and highly respected overseas. He has continually rejected Chinese invitations to move back home to live in Tibet. He continues to demand that Tibet be granted full independence.

In 1988, however, he changed this demand, suggesting that Tibet be allowed to govern itself in association with China. The following year, he was awarded the Nobel Peace Prize. It was given to him in recognition of his non-violent struggle for the liberation of his homeland.

TAKE TIME TO THINK

Imagine that you are a Tibetan Buddhist forced into exile and compelled to leave your home country. What do you think you would miss most by having to leave your homeland? What would you hope for most as you look into the future?

The Dalai Lama, an important Buddhist spiritual leader, receiving the Nobel Peace Prize.

OVER TO **YOU** ▶▶▶

1 The Dalai Lama, as a Buddhist, believes strongly in the use of non-violence. Do you think that it would have been better if he had led an armed uprising against the Chinese army?

2 Carry out some research of your own to find out more about the early choice of Tenzin Gyatso to be the 14th Dalai Lama. Then write a biographical sketch of him in those early years.

3 Imagine that you are the Dalai Lama. What do you think you would really want for your people and your home country, more than anything else?

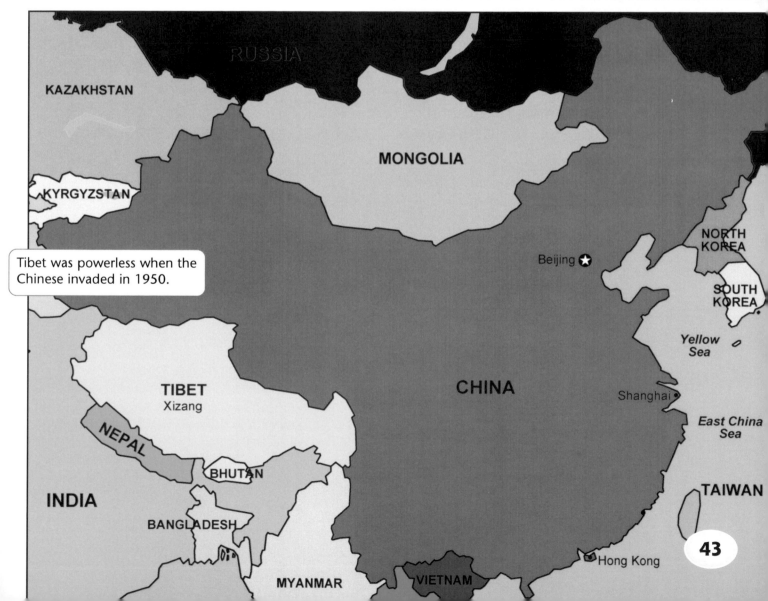

Tibet was powerless when the Chinese invaded in 1950.

For a Buddhist, getting married involves moving from one stage in life, that of being a student, to the next, that of being a householder. In the first of these stages, marriage is not considered to be suitable, although it is possible. It is more normal to wait until someone becomes a householder before marrying and starting a family.

BEING A HOUSEHOLDER

Householders are highly respected people in Buddhist society. The sangha of monks and nuns depends on them for its support and upkeep. In Theravada Buddhism, however, it is not thought likely that it will lead to enlightenment because being married involves taking on too many worldly distractions. At best, a married person can only hope to build up merit for a better rebirth in a future life. One of the ways of doing this is to support the monks and nuns by meeting some of their everyday needs.

BUDDHIST MARRIAGE

Buddhists believe that, although we influence one another, each person has their own individual karma. This means that two people, when they marry, cannot become as one person. Because of this, there is no distinct Buddhist wedding ceremony as such.

This does not mean, however, that Buddhists do not take marriage seriously. They do. Nor does it mean that Buddhists do not fall in love with each other just as other people do. They do.

Most wedding services involving Buddhists have two things in common:

- The bridegroom promises to love and respect his bride; to be kind and considerate; to be faithful to her; to trust her to run the household and to provide her with gifts throughout their married life to please her.

- The bride promises that she will perform her household duties efficiently; be hospitable to her in-laws and the friends of her husband; be faithful to her husband; protect the family's earnings and discharge her household duties lovingly.

These duties were first set out by the Buddha himself and have been unchanged ever since.

A *"May there ever be goodness, great riches and all life's necessities in their finest of forms; great joy, bliss and happiness, strength, good influence and the very best material life which is long enduring, free of sickness and wherein all one's wishes are fulfilled."*
Prayer from Samye Ling wedding service.

Although a Buddhist wedding can be led by a monk, this is not necessary.

SEX BEFORE MARRIAGE

As marriage is not believed by Buddhists to be a religious ceremony, so Buddhism does not teach that sex outside marriage is wrong. Buddhism, however, does teach that, if someone is in a relationship with another person, then they have a duty to be faithful to them. If they are unfaithful, then this is very hurtful to another person and can easily end up by destroying that relationship.

As far as sex before marriage is concerned, the Third Precept is against the misuse of sex. It is up to each person to decide whether sex before marriage is a misuse of the sexual drive or not.

DIVORCE

Buddhists do, of course, recognise that not all marriages are successful. They are prepared to support a divorce if this is thought to be absolutely necessary. They believe, however, that it is important that a divorce should cause as little hurt and distress as possible.

OVER TO YOU ▶▶▶

1 Copy out the two lists of the responsibilities that a Buddhist bridegroom and bride have towards each other.
   a) If you were making your own lists, which of these items would you change and which would you keep the same?
   b) Explain your reasons why.

2 Do you want to get married? If so, explain why. If not, explain why not.

3 Invent your own marriage service. Produce two readings that you would like included. What promises would you be happy making to your partner? What symbols might you include to make the service as meaningful as possible?

TAKE TIME TO THINK

Look at the division of responsibilities between the bride and the bridegroom. What clues can you find that this list was drawn up a long time ago?

AROUND BIRTH

You will find out

- The involvement of monks in ceremonies connected with birth.

- About the ceremony connected with birth.

- About the ceremony of shaving the baby's head.

In the glossary

Buddha

Mahayana Buddhism

Sangha

Theravada Buddhism

For Buddhists, the whole of life, including birth and the early years, are a preparation for the next rebirth.

Although Buddhist customs connected with birth and marriage vary from country to country, and between Mahayana and Theravada Buddhism, they often involved members of the monastic order – the sangha.

BIRTH

Whilst there are no Buddhist ceremonies that must be performed when a baby is born, monks are often invited into the parents' home to chant texts from the Buddhist scriptures – called paritta. In return for this, parents donate food or other gifts to the local sangha.

The child can also be taken along to the temple to be named. At this ceremony, a monk sprinkles water over the child before pronouncing a blessing over it, expressing the hope that it will have a happy life in the years ahead.

The union of the four elements – solidity, fluidity, heat and motion – is also symbolised at this ceremony by burning a pure wax candle and then allowing the melted wax to fall into a bowl of pure water. The coming together and uniting of the four elements symbolises that unity which, it is hoped, the child will achieve throughout its life.

SHAVING THE BABY'S HEAD

The main ceremonies for a Buddhist baby take place when it is about a month old. These take place in different stages:

- The baby's head is shaved. This is a reminder of the Buddha's teaching about life forces, which a person carries from one life to the next. The hair is a sign of a bad life force carried over from a previous life and so it is better for the baby if it is removed and destroyed.

- Special cotton is tied around the baby's wrists in the hope that it will bring him or her good luck.

- The baby is often given his or her name at this time.

BIRTH CEREMONIES AND THEIR IMPORTANCE

Buddhism teaches strongly that it is the way that a person lives which is most important. This is because of the emphasis that the religion places upon birth and rebirth.

For Buddhists, birth and rebirth are just stages on the journey of the soul to another life. This means that there are no fixed ceremonies in Buddhism. People living in different countries will celebrate such important events as birth and death in different ways.

The usual custom is to celebrate birth and death in the way that such events have always been celebrated in that country. This means, of course, that such Buddhist celebrations may be very different from one Buddhist country to another.

OVER TO YOU ▶▶▶

Imagine that you have a young baby. Devise a service/celebration that would best express what you hope for your baby and its future.

TAKE TIME TO THINK

Why do you think that so many Buddhist ceremonies involve monks?

BUDDHISM AND FAMILY LIFE

You will find out

- The importance of family life in Buddhism.

- The teaching of the Buddha about the responsibilities of husbands and wives to each other.

In the glossary

Buddha

The monk or nun who lives a celibate life, and so does not have a family of their own, is highly respected in Buddhism. He or she is given the task of teaching others and so helping them on their spiritual journey. At the same time, it is important to realise that the vast majority of Buddhists are neither monks nor nuns. They are ordinary men and women who marry and raise a family.

FAMILY LIFE

Although the Buddha had much to say about the life that he expected nuns and monks to follow, he also recognised that this would not be the way of life that most of his disciples would follow. This is one of the most important pieces of advice that he gave to them:

A **"**Support your parents.
Care for your wife and children.
Have a peaceful occupation.
This is the highest blessing.**"**

Buddhists believe that all family life should be built on the foundation of love but this is not love quite in the way that most of us think about it. A love which is based on the need to always be with someone is a selfish love, based on desire and attachment. Desire and attachment are one of the major contributory factors in suffering. True love in Buddhism is that which only thinks of the happiness of someone else. It only thinks about making someone else happy.

In a Buddhist family, the mother and father have clear responsibilities.

COUPLES AND THEIR RESPONSIBILITIES

The Buddha gave his followers advice on how husbands and wives should treat each other:

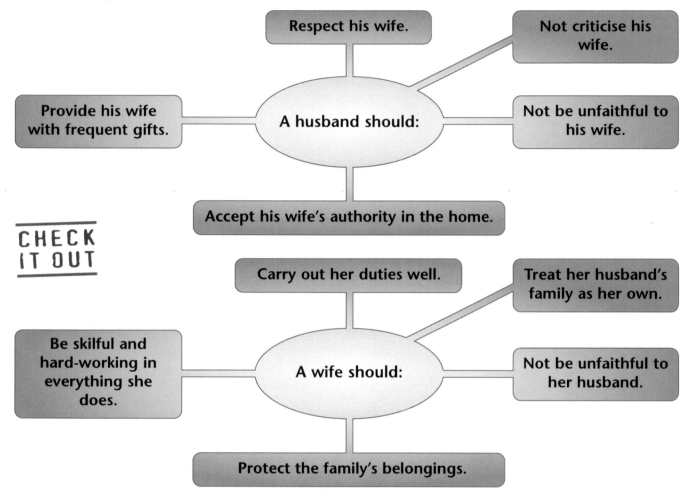

Respect his wife.

Not criticise his wife.

Provide his wife with frequent gifts.

A husband should:

Not be unfaithful to his wife.

Accept his wife's authority in the home.

CHECK IT OUT

Carry out her duties well.

Treat her husband's family as her own.

Be skilful and hard-working in everything she does.

A wife should:

Not be unfaithful to her husband.

Protect the family's belongings.

In one sense, Buddhists believe that everyone and everything have been our parents. You can see what an early Dalai Lama had to say about this in Extract B.

B *"There is no being we can say has not been our parent. In fact, each and every being has been our parent countless times."*

TAKE TIME TO THINK

What do you think about family life? Give three examples of ways in which you are glad that you belong to a family. Give three examples of reasons why you sometimes might question the value of family life.

OVER TO YOU ▶▶▶

1 Buddhists believe that true love only wants someone else to be happy. Why do you think that the love of a mother for her baby is usually held up as the perfect example of true love?

2 Look at Extract B. What do you think the Dalai Lama meant when he said that everyone, and everything, has been our parent?

3 Imagine you are a Buddhist who is just about to marry. How would you try to treat members of your new family in the right way?

A BUDDHIST FUNERAL

You will find out

- The Buddhist attitude when death arrives.
- The things that happen soon after death.
- The importance of relics.
- The way in which merit is gained.

In the glossary

Arhant

Buddha

Dana

Five Precepts

Karma

Monastery

Nibbana

Rupa

Stupa

Three Jewels

In one way, a Buddhist finds death easier to accept than the followers of any other religion. Throughout his or her spiritual life, a Buddhist has accepted the principle that all of life is impermanent and that decay is always at work. This is the clear teaching of Buddhism:

A "*Death carries off a man who is gathering life's flowers, whose mind is distracted, even as a flood carries off a sleeping village. All created things are impermanent. When one by wisdom realises this he heeds not this world of sorrow.*"

The Buddha

AT THE TIME OF DEATH AND AFTERWARDS

When the time to die arrives, the only attitude that a Buddhist can have is that of acceptance. The state of mind with which the last moments of life are faced is very important since this will determine a person's karma.

Friends, relations and monks gather around the deathbed of the person to help them. They carry out acts of devotion and recite passages from the Buddhist scriptures. Everyone present recites the Five Precepts and the Three Jewels.

In the days following death, several ceremonies take place:

- The ceremonies between death and cremation may last for three days. During this time, monks take the opportunity to remind everyone that life is impermanent. They also express the hope that the person will reach the blessed state of nibbana.

- Relatives and friends try to influence their progress towards nibbana by carrying out acts of **dana** [giving alms].

- Ceremonies carried out seven days, three months and annually after death are an attempt to transfer some merit to the dead person. The relatives try to do this by feeding the monks, giving them new robes and taking part in ceremonial water-washing rituals.

WHAT IS MERIT?

As we will see in Unit 25, Buddhists believe that the soul of each person is reborn many times. They believe that doing a good deed can help a person on their way to nibbana. This is why, when a person dies, their relatives and friends often give a gift to the monastery. They then ask that the merit they receive for making the gift should be shared with the dead person.

Celebrating different Buddhist festivals each year also has an important part to play in this. Ceremonies during these festivals are also an attempt to 'pass on' the merit to those who have died. Performing such ceremonies is a way of helping them.

A relic is often placed in a statue of the Buddha.

COLLECTING RELICS

If the person who has died is believed to have reached nibbana through becoming enlightened or is an **arhant** [saint], relics of the person are gathered together after the cremation. These relics can then be placed in a stupa or in a rupa. When a Buddhist comes across a stupa or sees a rupa in a temple or a house, he is reminded of the teachings of the Buddha.

TAKE TIME TO THINK

What do you think that the Buddha meant in Extract A when he likened death to the carrying-off of a man who is gathering life's flowers with a distracted mind? This is something for you to discuss with your partner.

OVER TO **YOU** ▶▶▶

1   Read Extract A carefully. Rewrite it in your own words to show that you understand what it is saying.

2   a) Explain what Buddhists mean when they speak of 'earning merit'.

    b) How might a Buddhist try to earn merit for someone who has died.

3   What happens to the bones [relics] of Buddhists who have died and reached nibbana?

4   What do you think a Buddhist might hope for at a person's funeral?

You will find out

- The importance of having the right attitude to death.

- The meaning of death for Buddhists.

- Illustrations to explain the Buddhist meaning of death.

- The meaning of 'nibbana'.

In the glossary

Buddha

Karma

Nibbana

Samsara

Siddartha Gautama

As we saw in Unit 24, Buddhism teaches the importance of having the right attitude to death. Death was one of the four 'signs' or experiences that prompted Siddhartha Gautama, who became the Buddha, to leave his palace and set off to find an answer to the problem of suffering. The Buddha taught that death is not something to be feared – it must be accepted.

A *"It is unsure whether tomorrow or the next life will come first."*

The Buddha

WHAT IS DEATH?

The Buddha taught that death is part of a continual process of change, decay and new life, which governs the whole of existence. This cycle of birth, death and rebirth is called samsara. You can find in Extract B a chant which is often sung by Buddhist monks at a funeral.

B *"All things in samsara [the world of life and death] are impermanent. To be happy there can be no clinging."*

Chant sung at Buddhist funerals

Buddhist funeral ceremonies provide an opportunity for people to reflect on the impermanence of life. Buddhists believe that people do not have a permanent soul that passes into another body at death. What, then, happens? To answer this question, two illustrations are often used:

- The passing of the flame from one candle to another at death. The question asked is whether the second candle burns with the same flame as the first candle or is it another flame altogether?

- The flowing of one river into another. The question then to be asked is whether it is the same river or has another, new, river been created?

The Buddhist answer is that neither the flame nor the river are static energies. They are ever-changing bundles of energy. The transfer of the flame from one to the other and of the water from one river to another is a transfer of energy. So, too, is the transfer of energy from one body to another at death.

The Buddha believed that things are reborn according to their karma. This word, meaning 'action', refers to the law of cause and effect. Every person suffers the consequences of their past actions.

WHAT IS NIBBANA?

A belief in rebirth has two consequences for this life:

- It encourages people to treat the whole world of nature with great respect. If an insect or a creature is annoying you then it is good to remember that it might be a relative or a close friend from a past life. If you kill it, you could be killing one of your relations.

- It encourages people to develop their own spiritual life so that they can return at a higher level in the next life.

The aim of every Buddhist is to escape from the cycle of samsara and to enter nibbana. Death is simply a stepping-stone on this journey. It may be the final stepping-stone or there may be many more to come. The word 'nibbana' means 'to blow out' as a flame is blown out. Nibbana is the eternal state that lies beyond all suffering. It is a state of eternal peace and happiness. It is the state where everything ceases – including all pain and suffering.

OVER TO YOU ▶▶▶

1 Write two sentences to explain what Buddhists mean by:
   a) Samsara
   b) Nibbana
   c) Karma
2 List three things that Buddhists believe about life after death.

TAKE TIME TO THINK

Buddhists believe that life is impermanent – as Extract B shows. What do you think they mean by this? What evidence do you think can be brought forward to support it?

Flowers are often used by Buddhists to show that life is short – and always ends in death.

We live in a very unfair and unequal world. It is divided into two parts – by wealth on the one hand and poverty on the other. We have:

- **The developed world.** This part of the world includes countries with a high standard of living, such as Western Europe, North America and Australasia. Although only 25% of the world's population lives in the developed world [about 1,700 million people], it consumes 80% of all the world's resources – especially energy and food.

- **The developing world.** These are countries with a low standard of living, including most of the countries of South America and Africa. These countries have 75% of the world's population but they have to manage on 20% of the world's resources.

What does Buddhism have to say and teach about creating a fairer world?

BUDDHISM AND A FAIRER WORLD

The Buddha was born into a very wealthy home but this did not make him happy. To find spiritual happiness, he tried living in extreme poverty, but this did not make him happy either.

The Buddha decided that a Middle Way between these two extremes of poverty and wealth was the only way to find spiritual satisfaction.

EXTREME WEALTH   **EXTREME POVERTY**

THE MIDDLE WAY

People need a certain amount of physical comfort but it is a spiritual disaster to spend all of one's life improving material comforts. Buddhism teaches that people who follow the Buddha's teaching must generously share what they have with others [A].

A   *"Cause the blind, the sick, the lowly, the protectorless, the wretched and the cripple equally to attain food and drink without interruption."*

Nararjuno, Early Buddhist teacher

Buddhists must give to anyone in need because by doing so:

- They build up their own good karma, so leading to a better rebirth.

- They help the person in need to think more deeply about the Buddha's teaching.

- They act with 'compassion' – an important Buddhist teaching.

TAKE TIME TO THINK

Someone has said: "Although the many charities channel a great deal of money and help to the poorest countries, this can never make the world really fair." What do you think they had in mind when they said this?

Buddhism teaches that people need a certain amount of comfort but to spend a life chasing after wealth is a great mistake.

THE KARUNA TRUST

Many Buddhists support the Karuna Trust. This is one practical way that they try to move towards a much fairer world. Since 1980, The Karuna Trust has worked with some of the most disadvantaged people in India. Most of these people come from the communities that, under the old Caste System, were called 'untouchable'. They are now normally called Dalits or 'oppressed' people. They were thought to be so inferior as human beings that mere contact with them 'polluted' other people.

Today, this group contains more than 150 million people. The Karuna Trust funds:

CHECK IT OUT

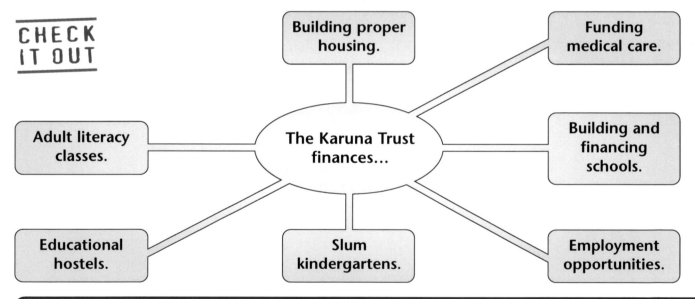

The Karuna Trust finances...

- Building proper housing.
- Funding medical care.
- Adult literacy classes.
- Building and financing schools.
- Educational hostels.
- Slum kindergartens.
- Employment opportunities.

OVER TO YOU ►►►

1 If you were to ask a Buddhist how he or she would go about creating a fairer world, what do you think they would say?

2 What do Buddhists mean when they talk about the 'Middle Way' and how might this help them to create a fairer world?

3 a) What work is carried out by the Karuna Trust.

  b) How do you think the work of charities like this helps to create a fairer world?

BUDDHISM AND SUFFERING

You will find out

- The different kinds of dissatisfaction or suffering in Buddhism.
- The story of Kisa Gotami.
- The Buddhist teaching about finding happiness.

In the glossary

Buddha

Dharma

Karma

The teachings of the Buddha started and ended with the problem of suffering. Ordinary life – from birth through life to death and rebirth – can hold no satisfaction for anyone. Everyone is dissatisfied with their existence.

There are eight kinds of dissatisfaction or suffering:

CHECK IT OUT

The suffering of being born.

The suffering of growing old.

The suffering of our own karma.

The suffering of sickness.

The eight kinds of suffering

The suffering of not getting what we want.

The suffering of death.

The suffering of unpleasant encounters.

The suffering of separation from loved ones and objects.

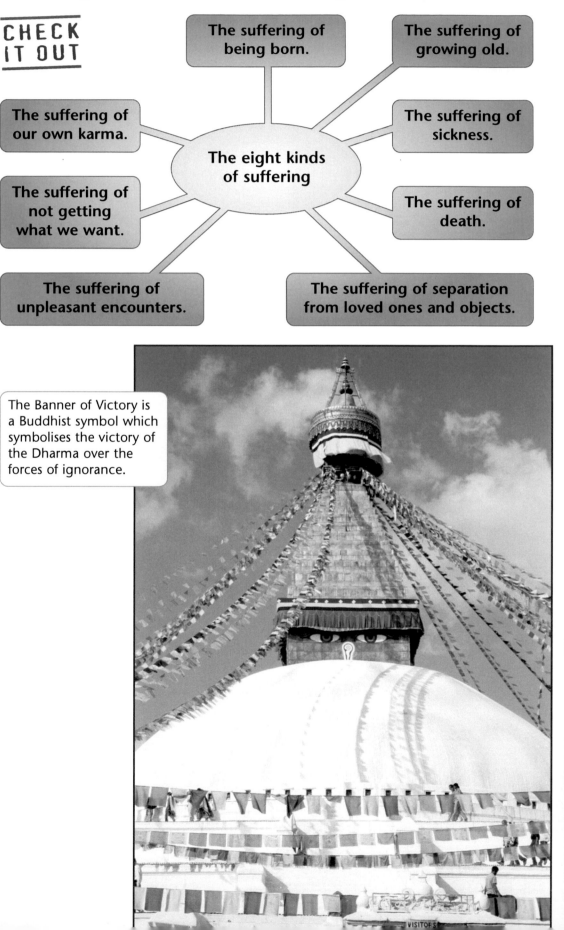

The Banner of Victory is a Buddhist symbol which symbolises the victory of the Dharma over the forces of ignorance.

THE STORY OF KISA GOTAMI

Buddhists believe that suffering is unavoidable and this is illustrated by this story:

Kisa Gotami had a much-loved son who suddenly fell ill and died when he was just one year old. Unable to accept her son's death, she took him in her arms and ran from house to house, seeking medicine to make him better. No one could help until someone suggested that it would be a good idea to consult the Buddha.

The Buddha told her to go to a family that had never known death and collect four mustard seeds from them. Kisa began her search. She was unable to find any such family. At last she saw that the Buddha was helping her to understand a most important lesson – that death touches everyone in some way. She took her dead son home and soon became a follower of the Buddha.

TAKE TIME TO THINK

Here is a rather puzzling little poem for you to think about:

B *"The village I reach at last*
Deeper than the deep mountains
What joy
The capital
Where I have always lived."
There is always a choice.
Great Zen Master Dogen

What 'capital' do you think he was talking about?

FINDING HAPPINESS

Buddhism teaches that people can overcome suffering and delusion. All suffering and its cure is in the mind. Although evil affects others it has its greatest impact on the person concerned. People must train their minds to overcome the obstacles to happiness. The first step to doing this is to recognise the First Noble Truth [see Unit 7].

There are many pleasures in life that people experience but these pleasures are unsatisfactory:

- The pleasures of this life never last.

- Even if a pleasure is enjoyed, the person always strives for more pleasure.

- There is always physical or mental suffering which destroys human pleasure [A].

A *"Using our present rebirth only to enjoy pleasures is like a dumb animal that eats the grass at the edge of a cliff, in constant danger of falling off."*
The Wishfulfilling Golden Sun.
Lama Zopa Rinpoche

Happiness, then, is an inner experience that is within all of us rather than something that always seems beyond us. The only way to find it is to follow the teaching [the Dharma] of the Buddha.

OVER TO YOU ▶▶▶

1 Look at the eight different kinds of suffering. What do you think are the worst forms of suffering that anyone can experience? Explain your reasons for your answer.

2 Do you think that the way in which Kisa Gotami discovered that everyone suffers was a good way for her to find out? Give one reason for your answer.

BUDDHISM AND PREJUDICE

You will find out

- About the deluded mind.

- The six major delusions of human beings.

- About overcoming prejudice.

In the glossary

Buddha

Enlightenment

Karma

Nibbana

Buddhists believe that all beings, not just humans, have within them the same Buddha Nature. This means that they have the same potential to be enlightened as the Buddha himself had. This Nature is obscured, to a greater or lesser extent, as clouds can block out the moon. It can be stained by defilements such as hatred, greed and delusion.

Buddhism teaches that any form of prejudice can be overcome.

OVER TO YOU ▶▶▶

Buddhism teaches that life is full of surprises. What do you think a Buddhist might learn from these two examples?

1   There is a story of a plump figure called Pu-Tai who lived in China in the 10ᵗʰ century CE. He spent his time telling stories and playing with children, or just sitting around, a combination of a tramp and a clown. It is rumoured that he was the Buddha Maitreva.

2   A Tibetan story tells of an ordinary villager, whose rainbow-light body after his death showed that he was an enlightened being, who spent his life working as a poor peasant farmer, happy at least that his son was a monk.

THE DELUDED MIND

Buddhism teaches that all problems stem from a deluded or deceived mind. This delusion was identified by the Buddha in the second Noble Truth as desire – the major cause of suffering. It is only when desire is extinguished that we will find true and lasting happiness:

CHECK IT OUT

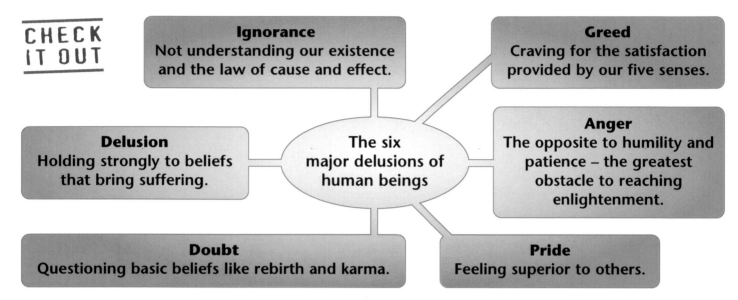

Ignorance
Not understanding our existence and the law of cause and effect.

Greed
Craving for the satisfaction provided by our five senses.

Delusion
Holding strongly to beliefs that bring suffering.

The six major delusions of human beings

Anger
The opposite to humility and patience – the greatest obstacle to reaching enlightenment.

Doubt
Questioning basic beliefs like rebirth and karma.

Pride
Feeling superior to others.

These delusions build barriers between people. They lead people to feel good about themselves and better than others. They lead people to want power over others. They encourage people to believe that their nationality, colour, intelligence and social position makes them better than others. Power, cleverness or wealth, far from being advantages, can be great disadvantages on the journey to nibbana. These feelings lead people to feel prejudiced towards others.

OVERCOMING PREJUDICE

How can any feelings of superiority and prejudice be overcome? Buddhists believe that they should:

- See themselves as equal to but no better than others. They must recognise what all human beings have in common. This advice was given by a Tibetan spiritual master:

A   *"All human beings have a wish in common. We wish to be happy and avoid suffering. Even newborn babies, animals and insects have this wish. It has been uppermost in our mind since beginningless time and is present even during our sleep. We spend our whole lives working very hard to fulfil this wish."*

Universal Compassion, Geshe Kelsang Gyatso

- Lay aside any feelings of superiority. The more enlightened a person is, the more they treat others as their equals. They show them the same love and respect that they show to their parents and children. There are Buddhist stories of human beings laying down their lives for animals while the Buddha showed respect for a prostitute with leprosy.

- Follow the example of those who have reached or are close to enlightenment.

TAKE TIME TO THINK

How do you think that people can overcome feelings of prejudice and superiority towards others – whether based on their sex or colour? How would you set about it?

THE ROLE OF WOMEN IN BUDDHISM

As in all religions, the teaching in Buddhism about the role of women reflects beliefs that were held at the time of the Buddha. There is often real tension between these views and those that are held by followers of the religion today.

THE ORDER OF NUNS IN BUDDHISM

One of the problems about the role of women in Buddhism is the way that the order of nuns, the sangha, was founded. The Buddhist scriptures tell how the Buddha's aunt wanted to become a nun but he was far from happy with the idea. Ananda, one of the Buddha's most devoted followers, intervened on her behalf.

Eventually the Buddha was persuaded to change his mind. He insisted, however, that she and other would-be nuns must meet two conditions:

- They must obey more monastic rules than the monks.
- They must place themselves under the authority of the monks, giving the strong impression that women are the inferior sex.

Over time, few women came forward for ordination and, in Theravada Buddhism, full ordination for women almost died out. Now women can only be ordained as novices. Many Buddhist women would like to see this changed. There is now an international Buddhist Women's Association that is arguing that change is long overdue.

The Buddha was reluctant to set up an order of nuns.

THE GOAL OF BUDDHIST WOMEN

From the beginning of Buddhism, there were two attitudes to women:

- In Theravada Buddhism, the goal of every woman was to be reborn as a man. In this life, however, women were encouraged to seek fulfilment through their role as mothers. Mothers were greatly honoured at the time of the Buddha and all Buddhists were encouraged to show the same loving kindness that a mother shows to her children.
- In Mahayana Buddhism, attitudes to women have always been much broader. They have been encouraged to undergo the same spiritual exercises as men. This is the story of Tenzin Palmo, a Buddhist woman who lived in the 20th century:

A   *"Anila Tenzin Palmo is an Englishwoman who came to India in 1964. While living in Dalhousie she helped with the Tibetan refugees and taught English to the Tulkus. Just after her 21st birthday in 1964 she became a nun. After she served as secretary to her lama for six years he sent her to meditate in the mountainous region of Lahul in India where she lived for 18 years. She lived in a monastery for the first six years before moving into a cave and has spent most of the last 12 years engaged in several retreats there, recently completing a three year solitary retreat."*

From Thebten Pemo 'Anila Tenzin Palmo' Mandala

There are many examples, from the time of the Buddha onwards, of Buddhist women who have reached enlightenment. Many Buddhists believe that more and more women will be used as spiritual teachers in the years ahead.

OVER TO **YOU** ▶▶▶

1   Write a letter to your friend, who has decided to become a Buddhist nun, trying to dissuade her from being ordained and taking robes because she will lose her freedom. Then write her response to your letter.

2   Someone has said that: "There is no clear teaching in Buddhism about the role that women should play in the religion." Do you agree? Explain your answer.

TAKE TIME TO THINK

If you held Buddhist beliefs about reincarnation and enlightenment, would you like to be reborn as a man or a woman in the next life? Give some reasons for your answer.

Everyone is now aware of the threats that many aspects of human behaviour present to our planet. We have:

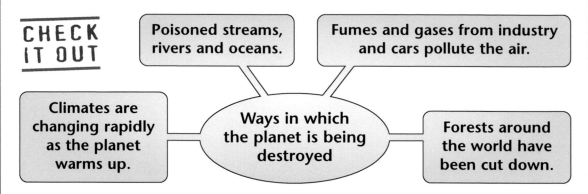

CHECK IT OUT

- Poisoned streams, rivers and oceans.
- Fumes and gases from industry and cars pollute the air.
- Climates are changing rapidly as the planet warms up.
- Ways in which the planet is being destroyed
- Forests around the world have been cut down.

There is not much in the Buddhist scriptures about environmental matters. This is because these were not important issues for early Buddhists. Even today, Buddhists are not particularly prominent in the battle to save the planet.

SENTIENT AND NON-SENTIENT BEINGS

Buddhism divides the whole of nature into:

Sentient beings

These are living, breathing beings who can feel, think and suffer. Buddhism stresses that all human and non-human life is dependent on each other. An illustration of this is the Buddhist custom in Thailand of buying fish and caged birds during the festival of Wesak and setting them free. Liberation and freedom are illustrated by these compassionate acts.

Non-sentient beings

This is the world of objects such as rocks and stones. Buddhists believe that the world is equally important because it can produce an atmosphere that helps wisdom to grow – well illustrated in the Japanese use of gardens as places of meditation.

THE BUDDHA AND COMPASSION

It is important to notice that:

- The Buddha tried to avoid harming plants, trees, insects and other seemingly insignificant parts of nature. Burning down trees and damaging plants were forbidden to the early Buddhist monks. The Buddhist Emperor Ashoka [268-239 BCE] outlawed the burning of forests unless there was a good reason for their destruction.

- Buddhists seek to protect plants and trees because of the sentient beings that live in and around them. They do so out of compassion. Obviously this includes the animals, insects and human beings that depend on them. In some Buddhist countries, spirits and gods are also believed to inhabit the area around non-sentient beings. In Tibet, for example, offerings to gods and spirits are made before a new building project gets underway.

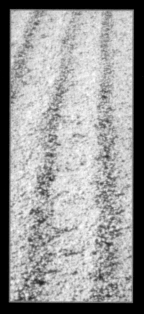

WHO IS RESPONSIBLE?

Some Buddhists are very critical of 'Western values', which they hold responsible for the environmental crisis – particularly the materialism which leads people to want more and more. They also point out that too many people want to 'conquer' nature rather than work alongside it. We still speak, for instance, of 'conquering' a mountain when we climb it.

To show that they are 'green', some Buddhists have become 'engaged' Buddhists. This means that they engage in direct action to protect the environment. Buddhist priests in Asian countries often run training classes, teaching other Buddhists to look after, and protect, the environment. Some monasteries have purchased land so that it can be reforested.

OVER TO YOU ▶▶▶

1 What is the difference between sentient and non-sentient beings?
2 Why do some Buddhists seek to protect plants and trees?
3 What is an 'engaged' Buddhist?

TAKE TIME TO THINK

What do you think a Buddhist might say about the lifestyle that you, your friends and your family follow? Do you think that he might have a point?

Buddhists value gardens very highly as places of deep peace and tranquillity.

BUDDHISM AND ANIMAL RIGHTS

You will find out

- The important Buddhist belief about not harming any form of life.

- The reasons why many Buddhists are vegetarians.

- The attitude of Buddhists towards vivisection.

In the glossary

Five Precepts

Karma

Nibbana

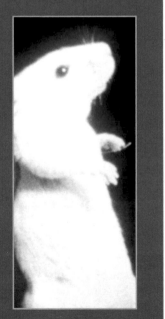

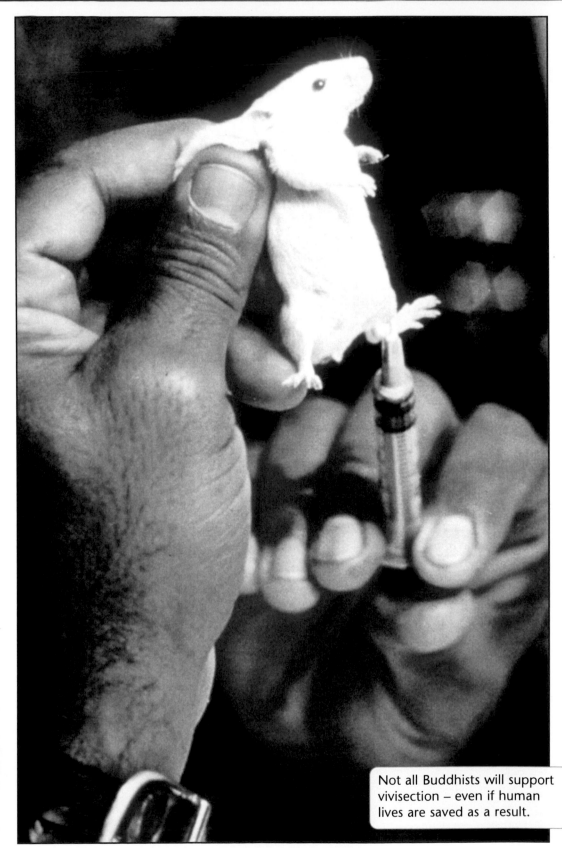

Not all Buddhists will support vivisection – even if human lives are saved as a result.

Do you remember the Five Precepts? If not, look back to Unit 10 to refresh your memory. You will see that all Buddhists are encouraged to make sure that they do not harm any human beings – and that includes being careful about what they say.

NOT HARMING ANIMALS

Buddhists are also encouraged to make sure that they do not harm animals. This has led many Buddhists to become vegetarians for the following reasons:

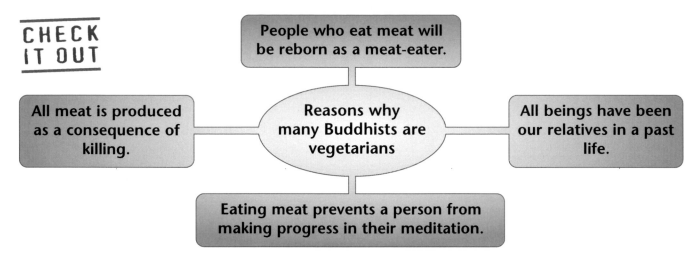

People who eat meat will be reborn as a meat-eater.

All meat is produced as a consequence of killing.

Reasons why many Buddhists are vegetarians

All beings have been our relatives in a past life.

Eating meat prevents a person from making progress in their meditation.

It is a fact, however, that not all Buddhists are vegetarians. One of the Buddhist holy books states that it is wrong to eat meat that has been specially killed for you. If you do, the only consequence can be bad karma. If, however, a person is not directly involved in the killing of the animal then it is perfectly acceptable for them to eat its meat.

VIVISECTION

Vivisection refers to experiments carried out on animals for medical research. About 2,500,000 such experiments are carried out in the UK each year. As this is only a recent practice, there is nothing in the Buddhist holy books to say whether this is a good thing – or not.

Buddhists do not agree about vivisection. They have two different attitudes:

1 It is a basic belief of Buddhism that it is wrong to kill any living thing. This must include the killing of animals in medical experiments – whatever the reason.

2 Medical and scientific experiments on animals are acceptable if certain conditions are met. They should be allowed if the lives of many human beings are going to be saved as a result. If these experiments are in the cause of the fight against disease then they can be justified. They cannot under any circumstances be justified, however, to develop better cosmetics.

OVER TO YOU ▶▶▶

1 A Buddhist made this comment: "There is no way that you can make any progress towards nibbana if you eat meat." How might a Buddhist argue to support this statement?

2 Suppose that you regularly buy your meat from a butcher or a supermarket. Does this actually involve you in killing the animal or not? What do you think?

3 Imagine a discussion between two Buddhists – one who supports the use of necessary medical experiments on animals and one who does not. Write down two arguments that each might use to support their case.

TAKE TIME TO THINK

Do you think that more people would become vegetarians if they had to kill the meat they ate themselves?

BUDDHISM AND WAR

You will find out

- The reasons why people and nations fall out with each other.
- The Buddhist way of tackling violence.
- Buddhism and pacifism.

In the glossary

Ahimsa

Five Precepts

Karma

Mahayana Buddhism

Theravada Buddhism

Many of the conflicts between nations in the world are caused by the same factors that lead people to fall out with each other:

CHECK IT OUT

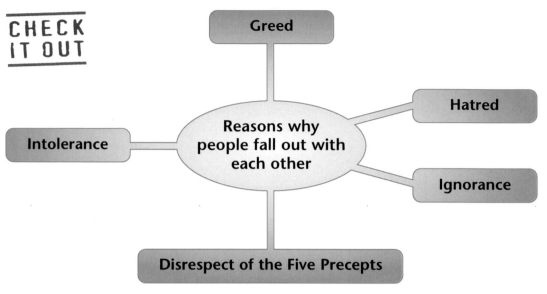

The ideal Buddhist attitude in this world is:

A *"Hatred is never appeased by hatred in this world: it is appeased by love."*

Radhakrishnan

TACKLING VIOLENCE

Since the first precept is non-harming [ahimsa], Buddhists obviously disapprove of violence. Take an actual example: A gunman breaks into a house and threatens the owner's family. How should they respond? Buddhists say that the gunman should be disarmed, without harming anyone while protecting the family. What, though, if the gunman is killed in the process?

- Theravada Buddhists say that killing is always wrong and has serious consequences for a person's karma.
- Mahayana Buddhists say that, if the intention is right, then no serious consequences for a person's karma take place.

The same principle holds true of violence between nations.

OVER TO **YOU ▶▶▶**

1 How would you try to solve the problem about the gunman referred to in the text. Would you feel that, if your life and that of your family were threatened, that any amount of force was justified?

2 a) What do you understand by the word 'pacifist'?

  b) Imagine that someone who is a pacifist is arguing with someone who isn't. What arguments do you think the two people would bring forward to support their case?

Most Buddhists are pacifists and do not believe in using violence in any situation.

BUDDHISTS AND PACIFISM

Buddhists tend towards pacifism and non-violence in all their dealings with other people. There is a strong Buddhist Peace Fellowship in the West and many Buddhists are still prepared to say with it: "It is better to be killed than kill…"

When looking at disagreements between nations, the important emphasis for a Buddhist is still the heart and mind of the individual – national action is a collection of individual actions:

B *"It hatred can be appeased by love and kindness on the individual scale surely it can be realised on the national and international scale too. Even in the case of a single person to meet hatred with kindness one must have tremendous courage, boldness, faith and confidence in moral force. May it not be even more so in international affairs?"*

Rahula, Buddhist teacher

Because of their experience of nuclear warfare in 1945, Japanese Buddhists are particularly active for peace. They have built peace pagodas in many parts of the world to remind people of the destruction that war brings.

TAKE TIME TO THINK

Do you think that it is realistic to adopt a pacifist attitude in the modern world? Perhaps it is the only possible attitude which offers the world any hope for the future? What do you think?

BUDDHISM AND SCIENCE

You will find out

- About scientific questions and Buddhism.
- About the Big Bang.
- The idea of continual creation.

In the glossary

Buddha

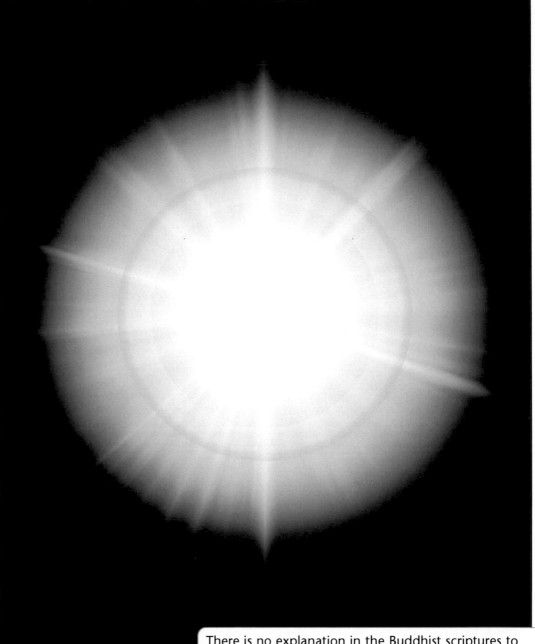

There is no explanation in the Buddhist scriptures to suggest that the world was created by a greater power.

Western religions such as Judaism, Christianity and Islam have often spoken of a conflict between their religious faith and science. The conflict has usually been over two issues:

- The age and the creation of the universe. Was the universe created by God in the 'recent' past? Was God involved in the work of creation? Is the universe much older than the religious stories of creation in the different holy books suggest?
- The appearance of human beings on the scene. When did the first human beings appear on Earth? Were they created by God? Were they created or did they evolve?

These are questions that have troubled religious people for a long time.

WHAT MIGHT A BUDDHIST HAVE TO SAY?

Alone among the major world religions, Buddhism does not have a story of creation. It does not even try to answer the question of how or why the universe was created. There is no Creator God in Buddhism and Buddhists do not believe that the universe was brought into existence by the creative activity of one supreme being. This makes it very different from Christianity, Judaism and Islam.

A BIG BANG OR NOT?

From the 1940s onwards, scientists have believed that the universe, and indeed the whole solar system, came into existence as the result of a massive explosion in space [the Big Bang]. As a result, matter was propelled through space at a phenomenal speed, but it gradually slowed down and cooled. Our universe was among the pieces of matter that cooled. The universe is still expanding, although its rate of doing so is slowing down.

Buddhists do not believe that the universe was created at a moment in time. They believe that the universe has always existed. It has always moved through four different ages:

- Creation
- Existence
- Destruction
- Emptiness

At the end of the time of existence, the universe begins to move towards its destruction. When this process is completed, all that remains is the place where the Buddha was enlightened – the 'Indestructable Seat'. At this stage, the Age of Emptiness begins. When this ends, a new Age of Creation begins. There is no limit to the number of times that this process can begin and end. Human beings simply need to realise that all life involves change. They simply need to try to make sense of the life that they are living.

Albert Einstein was one of the most important scientists of the 20th century. He commented that:

A *"If there is any religion that would cope with modern scientific needs it would be Buddhism."*

> ## OVER TO **YOU** ▶▶▶
>
> 1 "The Buddhist idea of eternal creation is so strange that we cannot learn anything from it." Do you agree with this comment? If not, describe one thing that we can learn from it.
> 2 The Buddha taught that to try to work out how the universe arose and how it will end can only lead to a sense of frustration. It is not the way to find peace. Do you agree with him?

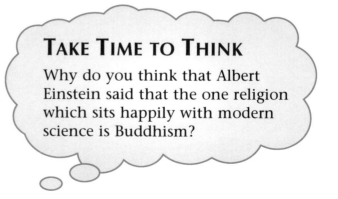

TAKE TIME TO THINK

Why do you think that Albert Einstein said that the one religion which sits happily with modern science is Buddhism?

GLOSSARY

Ahimsa: The Buddhist and Hindu belief that non-violence should be shown to all creatures – human and non-human.

Anatta: The belief that there is no permanent self.

Anicca: The belief that all things are impermanent.

Arhant: A 'worthy person', someone who has travelled the Noble Eight-Fold Path and has reached nibbana.

Benares: Town in India on the banks of the River Ganges, which is one of the most sacred Hindu pilgrimage sites.

Bhikkhu: A Buddhist priest.

Bodhissatva: A follower of the Buddha who was able to enter nibbana but chose to stay behind on Earth to teach others.

Brahman: The universal spirit in Hinduism.

Buddha: Title meaning 'the Enlightened One', given to Siddhartha Gautama after his enlightenment in 531 BCE.

Dana: Term used to describe the virtue of giving alms to the poor and needy.

Dharma: The teachings of the Buddha, one of the Three Refuges of Buddhism.

Dukkha: The heart of the teaching of the Buddha that everyone suffers.

Eight-Fold Path: The moral and spiritual training laid out in the Buddha's fourth Noble Truth, intended to lead to deliverance from suffering.

Enlightenment: State of consciousness where a person passes beyond the present world to eternal peace.

Five Precepts: The rules that all Buddhists are expected to follow.

Four Noble Truths: The set of principles through which the Buddha gained enlightenment.

Karma: The deeds or actions that determine a person's destiny in a future life.

Koan: A riddle that cannot be solved by the intellect.

Mantra: A sacred formula or chant.

Mahayana Buddhism: 'The Great Vehicle', the major branch of Buddhism, regards the Buddha as a superhuman figure.

Mara: The Evil One who tempted Siddhartha Gautama prior to his enlightenment.

Middle Way: The way in between extreme poverty and luxury that the Buddha encouraged his followers to pursue.

Monastery: The place where monks live, study and meditate.

Nibbana: [Also nirvana] Word means 'blowing out' or 'extinction', the state of bliss when enlightenment is reached.

Pali Canon: The scriptures of Theravada Buddhism.

Parable: A story that carries a religious or moral message.

Pilgrimage: A special journey taken to a site that is holy and sacred.

Reincarnation: The belief that some part of a person survives death and passes into another body.

Rupa: An image of the Buddha.

Samsara: The world of continuous change in which all human beings live.

Sangha: The institution of monks, founded by the Buddha, Buddhists say daily the words 'I go to the sangha for refuge'.

Siddhartha Gautama: The founder of Buddhism.

Skandha: The five parts that make up each human being – the body, feelings, perception, mental activities and the consciousness.

Stupa: A mount containing the remains of an important Buddhist religious figure.

Sutta Pitaka: One of the Three Baskets of scripture in the Pali Canon.

Ten Precepts: The ten rules which every Buddhist monk is obliged to follow.

Theravada Buddhism: Section of Buddhism that claims to follow the teachings of the Elders.

Three Baskets: Name given to the Pali Canon of Buddhist scriptures, otherwise known as the Tipitaka.

Three Jewels: Another name for the Three Refuges.

Three Refuges: The three things that each Buddhist takes refuge in – the Buddha, the teachings of the Buddha [the Dharma] and the sangha [the monastic community].

Tipitaka: See Three Baskets.

Uposatha Days: The practice of fasting or public confession in Buddhist communities, undertaken twice a month by monks.

Vihara: Term used in Buddhism to describe a building that houses a statue of the Buddha.

Yoga: 'Yoke', a method of self-control and meditation used by Buddhists and others.

Badger Learning
Suite G08, Business & Technology Centre
Bessemer Drive
Stevenage
Hertfordshire
SG1 2DX
Tel: 01438 791037
Fax: 01438 791036

Badger KS3 Religious Education
Buddhist Beliefs and Issues

First published 2007
ISBN 978-1-84691-086-9

Text © Michael Keene 2007
Complete work © Badger Publishing Limited 2007

Acknowledgements
   Photos © Alex Keene, The Walking Camera, with the following exceptions:
   2 Buddha (Hong Kong), 14 Buddha (Hong Kong), 24 Statue (Shanghai),
   27 Banner (Kathmandu) © Adam Wilmott.
   6 Olympic Flame, 20 Dalai Lama, 22 Child, 32 War © EMPICS.
   12 Wheel of Life © Simon Ferguson.
   16 Monks © Stone / Getty Images.
   17 Photographs and Dechen seal reproduced with the kind permission of Ganesha Press, ganesha@dechen.org.
   21 Wedding © Photo Resource Hawaii / Alamy.
   23 Family, 28 People, 30 Garden © Eye Ubiquitous / Hutchison.
   25 Flowers © Paul Martin Digital.
   29 Nuns, 31 Vivisection © Sipa Press / Rex Features.

Publisher: David Jamieson
Editor: Paul Martin
Designer: Adam Wilmott
Cover photo: Alex Keene
Illustrator: Juliet Breese and Adam Wilmott
Cover photo: Alex Keene, The Walking Camera